A PASTOR
IN EVERY PEW

A PASTOR
IN EVERY PEW

Equipping Laity for
Pastoral Care

Leroy Howe

JUDSON PRESS
PUBLISHERS SINCE 1824
VALLEY FORGE, PA

A Pastor in Every Pew
Equipping Laity for Pastoral Care
© 2000 by Judson Press, Valley Forge, PA 19482-0851
All rights reserved.

Bible quotations in this volume are from The Jerusalem Bible (JB), © 1966 by Darton, Longman & Todd, Ltd. and Doubleday and Company, Inc., and are used by permission of the publisher; the Revised English Bible (REB), copyright © Oxford University Press and Cambridge University Press 1989; the Holy Bible, King James Version (KJV); the *HOLY BIBLE: New International Version* (NIV), copyright © 1973, 1978, 1984. Used by permission of Zondervan Bible Publishers.

Library of Congress Cataloging-in-Publication Data
Howe, Leroy T., 1936-
    A Pastor in every pew : equipping laity for pastoral care / Leroy Howe.
        p. cm.
    ISBN 0-8170-1366-0 (pbk. : alk. paper)
        1. Laity. 2. Caring--Religious aspects--Christianity. 3. Church work. I. Title.

BV4400.H67 2000
253--dc21

00-038449

Printed in the U.S.A.
Third Printing, 2008

To Jennifer,
faithful shepherd
of the truth,

and Allison,
faithful shepherd
of the children

Contents

TRAINING MANUAL
A Program for Lay Shepherds

Preface

THIS BOOK IS ABOUT THE SPECIAL KIND OF CARING EXPRESSED BY PEOPLE of faith who want to be of help to others in the name of Jesus the Christ, the good and great Shepherd of all. I have written it for a body of caring persons who are willing to offer themselves to people in need but who from time to time question whether they have the requisite patience, character, insight, or skill to translate their sense of commitment into effective actions.

Most Christians I know already consider themselves to be full-fledged members of this special body. They want to offer a quality of caring that can make a positive, lasting difference to others in many different kinds of circumstances. However, fearing that their inadequacies could cause further suffering, they hesitate to share of themselves. This kind of hesitancy is both responsible and praiseworthy. If they are unable to bring about anything good in others' lives, they can respect them enough to avoid doing anything that will make the problems worse.

However, some of our reluctance as Christians to reach out to others comes from fears that are not well founded. For the message of the gospel is that "just as we are, without one plea," our loving Creator calls us to fellowship with him and service to others. And God has once and for all in Christ given us the example and the power we need in order to live as God desires us to live. Clarity about the example, trust in the power, and a healthy mindfulness about our limitations and sinfulness will take us a long way toward fulfilling our Lord's commandment to love others as he has loved us. In the process, our hesitation can be transformed into a confidence tempered by appropriate humility. In spite of our personal shortcomings, we can help others in Christ's name. God equips us for the task and blesses our efforts to complete it.

My primary purpose in writing this book is to show how ministering to others in the name of Christ can become a source of spiritual renewal for every Christian and of a contagious enthusiasm that can transform the life of congregations. Pastoral care is a ministry of all Christians, and as such it offers to every member of the Christian community the opportunity to share joyfully in Jesus Christ's self-giving for others, suffering and triumphing with him as God continues to work out loving purposes for the world.

Throughout this book, therefore, we will look at pastoral care as the work of every Christian and not just of the clergy. We will concentrate on caring in the name of Christ that is primarily person to person, or more specifically Christian to person, whether the recipient of the care is Christian or not. This book is about what goes on in effective encounters between caring Christians and those who are willing to risk being ministered to by them. But this book is also about Christian congregations as the primary environment of grace and power within which ministering in the name of Christ occurs.

The heart of the explorations to follow will be a close look at the ancient symbol of shepherding, long appealed to in the church as the most important concept for understanding what pastors do on behalf of others. My efforts will be directed at uncovering the richness of this symbol for expressing the caring ministry of laypersons. The result that I hope to accomplish is a useful guide for laymen and laywomen to shepherding others in the name of Jesus Christ and in the power of the Holy Spirit.

The first eight chapters center on the fundamentals of building any kind of caring relationship, as those fundamentals can be understood explicitly from a Christian point of view. The orientation of chapters 1 and 2 is that by becoming more caring of others in our hearts and by learning how to express that care through timely and effective actions on others' behalf, we will achieve the true humanness for which God has created us. The chapters following this discussion will focus, respectively, on the meaning of shepherding as it applies to lay ministers of care and on establishing the basic conditions for effective shepherding relationships in the context of a worshiping, praying, and caring congregation.

In chapters 9 through 17 we will concentrate on identifying the range of responses to people in need that Christian shepherds employ in common with all care providers, lay and professional. But throughout these chapters, we will also look at what makes Christian shepherds' uses of them distinctive from how other care providers, especially psychotherapists and counselors, apply them in their professional practices. For shepherds are not therapists or counselors. They are ministers. Chapters 18 and 19 explore two kinds of caring responses that are unique to the ministry of shepherding: prayer and Scripture reading. The final chapter shows how laypersons can enter into the ministry of shepherding with confidence and joy.

As a guide to Christian shepherding, this book can be read for general interest, and it can be used to train people for the ministry of lay pastoral care in Christian congregations. To facilitate both purposes, I have placed at the end of each chapter questions that are keyed to the issues discussed in that chapter. These questions can be the basis for each reader's reflection, as well as for discussion in groups. In either case readers will get more out of the questions by writing down their answers in journal form. Clergy and lay leaders interested in planning and carrying out a training program for shepherds in their congregations should read the training manual portion of this book first. There they will find a step-by-step guide to using the book for such a purpose.

Acknowledgments

T WO GROUPS OF DEEPLY COMMITTED CHRISTIAN MEN AND WOMEN contributed significantly to the writing of this book. The first group is composed of the several generations of pastoral care students that I have been privileged to teach at the Perkins School of Theology of Southern Methodist University. I am grateful for their sensitivity and insight as we sought a fuller understanding of the ministry of the laity in today's church and world.

The second group is composed of the lay ministers of pastoral care at First United Methodist Church, Richardson, Texas, with whom I have worked closely over the years. To my many requests for specific kinds of feedback they responded patiently and helpfully. Several of these capable shepherds reviewed earlier drafts of this book's chapters. They encouraged me when they thought I was on target and informed me when they thought I was not. For their encouragement and candor, my heartfelt thanks go especially to Sylvia Deadwyler, Marilyn Evans and Walter Evans, Chris Guldi, Bonnie Hegler, Nancy Howe, Bob Macy and Jean Macy, and Rae Taylor. Nancy, my wife, best friend, and favorite editor, cheerfully guided the process of the final reworking and rewriting.

All of us at the church owe a special word of appreciation to its senior pastor, R. David Shawver, for the unfailing support he continues to give his lay shepherds. David makes it easier for us to see what good shepherding can be like.

1. It's Lonely Out There

What is a frail mortal, that you should be mindful of him,
a human being, that you should care for him?
(Psalm 8:4, REB)

PSALM 8 CONTAINS ONE OF THE MOST IMPORTANT QUESTIONS ASKED anywhere in the Bible. And it is one of the most important questions any of us can ask about ourselves. Who are we? Where have we come from, and where are we going? In a violent world filled with frightened, lonely, defensive, and destructive people, do we have any reasonable prospects for a better future? Does anyone care?

The hymn that we know as the eighth psalm was sung at night in ancient Israel by worshipers who could see the stars shining down on the open courtyards of Solomon's temple. The view must have been extraordinary:

When I consider thy heavens, the work of thy fingers, the moon and the stars which thou hast ordained ... (Psalm 8:3, KJV)

The words inspired by the view contrast the majesty of God and creation with the fragility of human beings, while also declaring us to be "little lower than the angels" *(Psalm 8:5, KJV)*. What is important about us, however, is not our high station but that God remains "mindful" of us. God not only "spare[s] a thought" for us *(Psalm 8:4, JB)* but also cares for us. We are not alone. We matter—to the Maker of the heavens and the earth.

WHO AND WHOSE WE ARE

Though Christians are surrounded by other people who have all sorts of opinions about our nature and destiny on earth, our faith reminds us constantly of who we are. We are creatures of God called to live in a world governed from first to last by the love of God, with a nature resembling God's own. We are "crowned with glory and splendor" (*Psalm 8:5,* JB). Because we are, the possibility of living with gratitude to God and with respect, care, and love toward our family members, our neighbors, and our fellow inhabitants of the planet is indestructibly fixed in our hearts and minds. Because we are created for fellowship with God and one another, loving God and caring for one another can become the most natural of things to do.

Nothing that we as Christians say to anyone may be more important than emphasizing the love of God. The deepest need all human beings share is the need to be cared about by God and to care about others in God's name. So much that is happening in society should make plain the importance of the Christian message about our humanness.

WHAT WE ARE COMING TO

Much of what we hear sounds good: supporting family values, strengthening communities, making the environment healthier, revering multicultural, multiracial, and multireligious diversity, and seeking justice for all. If these things really do matter to most people, then we have reason to be hopeful. But on just these matters we experience the greatest difficulties making progress. The values that have become dominant in society point in another direction, toward harsher competitiveness and mindless acquisitiveness. Winning is better than losing, having more things is better than having few, and it is better that we rather than others be secure and comfortable. We recognize other people's presence and rights, but only when we have to.

Underlying all of these dehumanizing values is a full-blown paranoia about the paucity of good things in the face of others' claims to them. There is some ground for this paranoia: our planet's resources are shrinking in the face of ever-increasing population. What is most frightening about this prospect, however, is that many people see in it only personal meaning: their own aspirations and possibilities for success are at risk. They have little concern that the coming scarcity will affect the well being of everybody else. Their only question is "Will there be enough for me?" And how much is enough? We know the answer to this latter question, even though it is hard to admit: "enough" always means more than I now have.

In the moral quagmire of radical individualism, we are co-opted early for selfish purposes, and our worth is calculated in terms of our usefulness to someone else. Whether with store clerks, business partners, or family members, relationships are quickly reduced to merely functional value. We maintain them because we need what we can get for ourselves from them, whether it is a loaf of bread and a quart of milk, stock options, or a place to call home. When a relationship no longer serves our interests, we feel that we have the right to end it, unilaterally. Nowadays some marriage partners make a commitment to live together for only as long as love lasts.

Though our society is utilitarian in outlook, valuing everything in terms of how well personal interests are served, we maintain the vestiges of being a polite society. In some quarters, relationships with people have the appearance of being courteous and civil, even to the point of seeming respectful. But below the surface, being nice substitutes for caring. And even the niceness threatens to collapse from moment to moment. Hell is— other people, as Sartre once wrote, and most of them (never us) are like plumbers who overcharge, managers who reward only their cronies, and insatiable children who extort candy in the check-out line from harried parents too weary to protest.

WHAT PEOPLE NEED MOST

Is it any wonder, then, that there is such a desperate hunger for relationships in which people can count on one another, no matter what? Such relationships are rare. Some people are too needy themselves to be very caring of anyone else. Others live in environments too hostile to risk investing much of themselves in others' problems, hopes, and dreams. Still more are bewitched by our culture's exaltation of selfishness masked as a pursuit of self-realization, self-fulfillment, and authenticity. In spite of people's inability and unwillingness to enter into and stay in genuinely caring relationships, the hunger remains. It is a hunger that only a caring relationship can satisfy. And, thanks be to God, many people for whom self-satisfaction had been the norm of existence have begun to reach out for what genuinely caring people have to offer. Will Christian congregations be prepared to meet those people's needs?

We must hope so, for this yearning for close, genuine relationships can make Christian communities especially rich blessings to people in our time. A clearly stated promise in the name of the Christian gospel—that people will find caring relationships in our churches—plays an important, and sometimes the most important role, in many people's decisions either to join a church or to affiliate with one congregation rather than another. When the promise is fulfilled, what will our society's lonely, frightened, and weary people find?

In truly caring Christian fellowships, they will find themselves surrounded by people with an uncommonly high awareness of and sensitivity to their needs, longings, aspirations, and struggles. They will find themselves cherished and respected by people who accept them as they are and who do not try to remake them into someone else. They will be honored and supported as they seek God's will for their lives by people who give of themselves unstintingly and without calculations of appropriate paybacks. They will discover that they matter deeply to others, and in so doing they will learn how deeply they matter to God.

HOW WE CAN HELP

In a social order populated increasingly by the self-serving, there are still people around for whom life means more than getting theirs before it is gone, more than living in perpetual fear of being left behind, and more than doing unto others what they fear others are about to do to them. Against the banality of life on the cutting edge stand those who know a better way. That way is the way of committed, caring relationships for which personal sacrifices are made as a matter of course and within which the good of the relationship remains inseparable from the goods realized in the relationship. Only this way leads to fulfillment and joy in life. Here is where we come in, as shepherds in committed and caring congregations. We can be especially powerful witnesses to that better way of life that God in Christ has promised all of us in abundance.

Does this mean that as lay shepherds we must become better persons and better Christians than anyone else? Hardly. What God requires of us is more modest. Paul wrote to the congregation at Rome, "Do not think too highly of yourself, but form a sober estimate based on the measure of faith that God has dealt to each of you" (Romans 12:3, REB). Our relationships lack genuine caring because we become more preoccupied with ourselves and with what we can get from others rather than with what we must give in order to make our relationships truly fulfilling for all parties. We come to think more highly of ourselves than we think of our partners in the relationships. When we do, we inevitably begin to form judgments of them based on our assessment of what they can do for us.

Sometimes this happens even in the caring relationships offered by lay shepherds. For example, we can begin to put subtle pressure on a care receiver to solve his or her problem our way because we think more highly of our way than we should. When the care receiver is politely unresponsive to our pressuring, we may become frustrated and even irritated that our work is not producing the results for which it was undertaken. But we have not been invited into that other person's life in order to make our life more interesting or rewarding. Whatever personal satisfaction we may gain by doing good and doing it well must remain distantly secondary to staying focused on what the other person needs from us and to valuing the other's needs more highly than we value our own. In the kingdom of God, all relationships would be like this. For now, it will have to do to offer others a kind of care that can point to that kingdom in hope. That care begins with one person's sacrificing for the sake of another.

From the standpoint of faith, genuine caring is grounded in affirming others as persons of sacred worth, loved by God and destined for a future of God's making. The shape of our caring is anticipated in the life and ministry of Jesus Christ. Caring means serving God's desire and design for the other, helping the other to become the best that he or she is capable of becoming, in God's sight. By contrast, in today's narcissistic culture, people ask fervently: "How can I be sure that I will get what I want?" The more important question to ask about life is "How shall I remain open to sacrificing for others and at the same time grow to become the kind of person God wants me to become?" The answer to this question inevitably takes the form of a paradox: people who care about each other, genuinely and mutually, will find themselves by losing themselves for the sake of the other and for the Christ in the other.

In spite of this profound spiritual truth about life, however, many people scoff at the notion of sacrificial relationships. What everyone needs to cultivate these days, they think, is the shrewdness to get as much as possible from others and to move on when the payoff begins to diminish. Caring people are taken advantage of sometimes. But the far greater problem confronting us is the anxiety, loneliness, and despair that overwhelm life. The only lasting solution to this problem is through doing what the self-centered scoff at: putting others' well being above one's own. The scoffers are right to point out relationships in which there is too much you and not enough me. There are a lot of takers in the world who never seem to want to give back, for whom continued self-giving on the part of others can make it even more difficult to confront God's plan for their lives. Shepherding sometimes brings one face to face with such people, and learning how to deal with them lovingly but firmly can be an ordeal.

But deal with them we must. The self-sacrifice our Lord calls from us is not for the sake of others' ill-considered impulses and selfish whims. It is for the sake of others' becoming the unique persons God wants and needs them to be. To this extent, the scoffers force us to deal with a problem that every caregiver finds it necessary to confront: the threat of being exploited. But they are wrong in their insistence that the genuinely needy learn to take care of their own stuff and leave the rest of us out of it.

The basic premise of the scoffers is that all human values and dispositions are grounded in self-interest. For them, this means that genuine, caring relationships involving mutual self-giving can occur only sporadically at best. They are temporary arrangements threatened with engulfment in the tides of egocentrism that buffet our spiritual shorelines. Is this all there is to caring?

Not in many families, at least. However strong the pressures are to become caught up in the frantic pursuit of security, comfort, and possessions at others' expense, many families succeed at overcoming them. The parents in such families put higher values first and are the happier for it. They delight in rearing their children with love to become loving persons in their own right. Among these family members' greatest joys is finding ways to involve themselves meaningfully with others and to contribute positively to those others' well being. The difference they want to make in the world has less to do with having more than it does to serving more. For families like these, caring relationships are not accidents. They are the sum and substance of life.

This is true for many communities of faith as well. Congregations in which such caring families and caring relationships abound are truly blessed, and the abundant life that pours from their members is a blessing beyond measure to all whose lives they touch. To be sure, most congregations are not like this at the beginning. Early in their development, their leaders tend to be overwhelmed with the myriad details that must be attended to if they are to create a church: finding a place to meet and a site on which to build, informing people in the neighborhoods to be served, recruiting volunteers, securing judicatory approval and ongoing support, selecting a minister, developing age- and stage-specific programs, and on and on. Getting the people to the meetings and the payments to the creditors consume a great deal of the available energy at the start. Somehow, though, healthy congregations find a way early on to address the deeper and abiding questions of church life: who is it whose Word we proclaim, to whom shall we proclaim it, and for what ends? In their growing membership people grapple with the question of how their church, at this time and in this place, shall truly care for those entrusted to it by God.

What goes on all the time in caring families and in caring congregations is a powerful rebuttal to the cynicism of both the aggressive and the defeated whose lives are swallowed up in bitter platitudes: "nice guys finish last," "get yours before it's all gone," "watch your backside," "never trust anyone, period," or "to the victors belong the spoils." Theirs is a truly horrific vision of life. It is, in the fullest sense of the word, diabolical to the core, cutting people off from the genuine wellsprings of meaning, wholeness, and joy that flow everlastingly from the enduring mercies of God that are ever faithful and ever sure. The vision that our faith has to offer is something else entirely. It is a vision of caring communities with no boundaries and no end, praising God and enjoying God and each other, forever. We can have an important part in sharing that vision with others. As we share it by acting caringly on another's behalf, we will find ourselves increasingly caught up in it. There is no better place to be, in this life and in the life to come.

SOME QUESTIONS TO THINK ABOUT

1. What was the loneliest moment or time in your life? What made it so lonely for you? What helped you the most to get through it?
2. How would you express the difference between being alone and being lonely?
3. What are the most important things that life has taught you about how to express and how not to express care to a lonely person?
4. Have you ever felt taken advantage of when you reached out to someone in order to be of help? How did you deal with those feelings at the time? How can you be genuinely caring of someone who is demanding without letting yourself be taken advantage of (again)?

2. What Caring People Are Like

Look on my right and see,
there is no one to befriend me.
All help is denied me,
no one cares about me.
(Psalm 142:4, JB)

I thank God for putting into Titus' heart the same concern for you
that I have myself. (2 Corinthians 8:16, JB)

IN THE PREVIOUS CHAPTER WE LOOKED AT SOME OF THE MOST SIGNIFICANT characteristics of caring relationships and the desperate hunger for them that so many people experience. As a favorite song expressed it some years ago, "what the world needs now is love, sweet love." Whatever the song's writer might have had in mind as a definition for love, we can be clear that love includes a deep awareness of and sensitivity to another's needs, respect of his or her personhood as a gift from God, and a willingness to make significant sacrifices for the other's well being. Relationships in which these qualities are present are among the greatest blessings God has to offer us, in this life and in the next. And the people who can sustain them are as remarkable as the relationships their caring spirits bring about. What such people are like is the subject of this chapter.

Caring people show us an astonishingly different way of thinking, feeling, and acting than most of us see in all too many of our associations. They make palpable the vision of "new creation" that Paul shared with the church at Corinth (2 Corinthians 5:17). In their presence, old things do pass away and all things can become new. When a caring person is with us in our distress, the debilitating sameness of our lives begins to give way to hope that things can be different and better in all our relationships and that our attempts to make it so will be worth the effort. Caring people are wonderful to be around, because they are filled with wonder at the grace and the possibilities that God constantly offers us out of boundless love.

QUALITIES OF A CARING PERSON

Several inner qualities stand out in caring people. The first quality is an attitude of PROTECTIVENESS toward others, a sense of solicitude for their safety and their opportunities. The oft-used parting phrase, "take care," expresses the trait when it is said genuinely and not merely ritualistically. "Take care" captures that sense of concern about the other in a world we know to be filled with threat and promise. It conveys our profound hope that the other will come to no harm. When we take care in regarding another, we commit to do no harm. Caring persons, like parents, share a fundamental responsibility for the safety of those in their care. They protect others' well being, especially in situations fraught with risk and danger, just as good parents are especially watchful when their children are most vulnerable. Caring people do not typically find it difficult to assume a quasi-parental role with others at such times, but they also know that eventually they must move beyond that role if those they care about are to become the persons God intends for them to be.

For many people, the previous paragraph will sound as if it confuses caregiving with caretaking, particularly in the positive connotation assigned to the word *parental*. This association may even arouse suspicion and hostility. To some extent, such feelings are appropriate. Protectiveness can easily devolve into an inappropriate insulation from what people most need in order to grow: experimenting, taking risks, and learning from mistakes. Anxiety about keeping people safe can inadvertently bring into play a power structure that takes over others' right to choose for themselves. It does not seem to matter whether the head of the system is an autocratic priest, pastor, or bishop, a therapist who mistakes himself or herself for a shaman, or a physician who is considered beyond anyone else's questioning by virtue of specialized training and experience. However corruptible any would-be protector may be, nothing about a protective attitude necessarily leads to violating the rights and dignity of those needing the protection.

There is a close connection between a protective attitude and another important inner characteristic of caregivers: their acceptance of LEADER-SHIP responsibilities for guiding others toward worthy goals and away from what would be harmful to them. Caring about another includes desiring and actively contributing to what is genuinely in that other's best interest. This kind of care cannot be effective without the caring person's daring to envision a good or even a best for another. It takes courage to do this, for we hear too often the belligerent question, "Who are you to suppose that you could know what's best for anyone else?"

It is presumptuous to assume to know what might be better or best for another. And there is considerable risk involved in acting upon such knowledge. The helping act may be rejected, and so may the person offering the help. Or the caregiver might not acknowledge the rejection and act instead as if no is never an answer and holding back is tantamount to giving up. Perhaps even more dangerous is the possibility that efforts to lead others to new experiences, goals, commitments, relationships, and deeper faith will be received so warmly that the caregivers will come to believe more strongly in their insights and persuasiveness than they have any right to believe. In that case, their leadership takes on a smug, even condescending air that becomes increasingly offensive and stifling.

All of these considerations should remind us constantly of the vulnerability that a caregiver assumes whenever he or she takes on a guiding role in someone else's life. They also remind us that caregivers do lead and guide others. They act from an inner conviction that leading and guiding can be desirable and necessary. And they do not hesitate to do whatever is necessary to make a wider range of choices possible for those in their care and to share their conviction that some choices are better than others. In all of this, however, they respect the right and the importance of others to choose worthy goals for themselves.

This latter observation points to another characteristic of the caring attitude: SUPPORTIVENESS of the worthiness and the integrity of the other as a person in his or her own right. As therapists have come to understand it, supportiveness refers to those qualities of warmth, empathy, and unconditional positive regard necessary for the development of therapeutic relationships. It refers to respect for the right, the capacity, and the responsibility of others to work out solutions to their problems by themselves. Acts purporting to be helpful to others that do not affirm and support those persons as centers of value, meaning, power, intentionality, and responsibility cannot be truly caring acts, for there would be no caring spirit behind them.

One of the most widespread manifestations of helping without being supportive is in the area of caring for the poor: the children of the poor, the homeless poor, and the homeless mentally ill. In the United States the gap between the wealthy and the poor continues to widen. Government at every level continues to seek a way out of the morass of caring for the poor at the very time that it has become obvious to experienced volunteers that only government can carry out strategies on a large enough scale to help. Everywhere we turn, the poor have become merely part of the problem of poverty in our time, nameless obstacles in the struggles of the privileged for a better society on their terms.

Long ago, an unnamed woman entered a gathering at the house of Simon in Bethany and surprised the guests by pouring a bottle of very costly perfume over the head of Jesus, as if to anoint him for burial. Her astonishing act stimulated a discussion about waste that has been easily misconstrued for almost two thousand years. Many in the room at Simon's house conjectured that the money spent on the perfume could have been used to benefit the poor, "You have the poor among you always," Jesus said to the disciples, "but you will not always have me" (Mark 14:7, JB) And so the church supposedly has it on the Lord's authority that deploying hard-earned resources in profligate ways, perhaps especially for religious and spiritual purposes, is a praiseworthy act even at the expense of the suffering poor.

Evidently this story had considerable impact in the first century; each of the four Gospels relays a version of it. Luke seems to know of it, however, in the context of a discussion about sin and forgiveness rather than about providing for the poor (Luke 7:36-50). John (12:1-8) and Matthew (26:6-13) present the story in the way that Mark does. They both omit a critical additional remark by Jesus that occurs in the middle of Mark 14:7 (REB), "and you can help [the poor] whenever you like." Disconnected from its proper Old Testament context, Jesus' words become curious: at best, they suggest only a permission to be mindful of the poor. However, the larger context for these words is best expressed in Deuteronomy 15:7-11. The last verse is especially important: "The poor will always be with you in your land, and that is why I command you to be open-handed towards any of your countrymen there who are in poverty and need" (REB). Caring for the hungry, the thirsty, the stranger, the naked, the sick, and the prisoner

(*Matthew* 25:35-36)—for the poor, the blind, and the victimized (*Luke* 4:18-19)—is the heart and soul of a life lived in faithful response to Jesus Christ's call to discipleship in his name. Such caring proceeds from gratitude for a bounty that is the Lord's and not of our own making.

A final quality important to caring is the quality of being ENCOURAGING. The unexpected crises, hardships, and challenges that can bring out the best in us also can fill us with fears, drain our resources, shake our self-confidence, and raise doubts about whether we should hope for anything better. Strangely, things may be little better even when our changing circumstances have to do with things for which we have waited eagerly and prepared thoroughly. Opportunity no less than danger provokes insecurity, worry, and what can become a debilitating sense of aloneness.

Courage can fail us at any time in life, whether we are about to be overcome by something threatening or by something offering us exciting new possibilities. Caring people seem to know this as if by instinct. They seem to be able to discern just when to say "it's going to get better," "you're doing just fine," "hang in there," "you can do it," and perhaps most important of all, "I'm here." They seem to have a second sense about the power of touch and about the ways we have found to mistrust it, to our great pain. They know how to lend another some of their own courage without violating the other's right to face situations on her or his own.

Sometimes we think of this kind of caregiving as comforting. The idea is closely akin to one of our most powerful images of pastoral work: comforting the afflicted. Comforting in this sense involves soothing, calming, and reassuring. The word itself, however, suggests all this and more, most especially strengthening people. To comfort does mean to soothe, but it also means to hearten (cum fortis, with heart). As soothing addresses our feelings, heartening addresses our will and attitude—the state of mind with which we will approach what we must face. Encouragement helps people to overcome fear and to find strength in times of need. In sum, then, caring people protect, guide, support, and encourage.

CARING RELATIONSHIPS AND ATTITUDES

In these two chapters we have explored the meanings of care and caring by means of a distinction between care as a quality of relationships and care as an inner attitude exhibited by people in those relationships. In both senses of the word, care embodies the central affirmation of the Christian tradition about how we are to live in the world that God has created and asks us to tend. In the words of the Great Commandment, we are to love God totally and to love our neighbors as we love ourselves. The difference that Christianity has sought to make in the world is to show all humankind the meaning, truth, power, and ultimacy of the love of God the Creator, manifested wholly and completely in Jesus Christ. Can we not say, now, that care makes this kind of love incarnate? If love is the commitment and action that intends the well being of all God's creatures, then care is a relationship and an attitude in which God's love in Christ becomes embodied to everyone.

Around the distinction between a caring relationship and a caring attitude, however, revolves a final question, that of priority. If care is relational and attitudinal, are they co-equal in significance, or might one be more basic and in that sense foundational to the other? Another way of putting the question is "Which comes first—doing something for another person or being caringly disposed toward that person?"

Not one of these questions is important or interesting enough to pursue. And yet, untold energies have been dissipated over trying to settle the relationship between inner disposition and outward behavior. Do we become more caring in our relationships by cultivating a more caring attitude? Or do we become more caring inwardly by being consistently more caring toward others in our actions? However interesting such speculative questions may be to some—strategists for the causes of evangelism and social action in our churches come to mind immediately—the questions have little if any bearing on the practice of shepherding. For the purpose of nurturing others, it is enough to stand for cultivating both, in whatever order.

Sometimes we find it hard to be effective in caring for someone who is difficult to tolerate until we can find it within ourselves to look caringly upon him or her in spite of our feelings to the contrary. But at other times, it may take a series of caring actions on our part, even with teeth clenched, to bring about a newly caring disposition toward another. In both sets of circumstances, we may be surprised at how far we can come in changing our pattern of acting by working on our attitude, and in changing our attitude by acting when we would rather not. It is not necessary to have a fully operational theory about how this happens in order to trust that things will happen for the better in our attitudes and our relationships, however we may begin the process of making it happen. God will be there for us, wherever we may choose to start.

What has been written to this point, though it is shaped without apology by Christian terminology, nevertheless represents an understanding of caring that can be and is affirmed by care providers of diverse perspectives, both religious and humanistic. From here on, however, we will consider lay caregiving in explicitly Christian terms. The discussion will center upon a central image that the Christian tradition has consistently used to express its understanding of the kind of care God desires for his people: the image of shepherding. The sources of this image lie deep within the faith of ancient Israel as well. For both Jews and Christians, caring for people in God's name is like shepherding them. The God of Abraham, Isaac, and Jacob, fully incarnate in Jesus Christ, is consistently described in the Scriptures of Judaism and Christianity as a shepherd. And so the principal caregivers in the Christian community, pastors and people, may be described as shepherds. What the image of shepherd can mean to our understanding and rendering of lay caring ministries is the subject of the next chapter.

SOME QUESTIONS TO THINK ABOUT

1. Think about someone who played an especially caring role in your life. How would you describe that person to someone else?
2. How much like that person are you?
3. What is it like to protect, guide, support, or encourage someone too much? How can we prevent it from happening while we continue to care for that person?
4. In showing care to another person, what comes easiest for you? protecting? guiding? supporting? encouraging? What comes harder? What could you do to make easier the hard part?

3. The Christian as Shepherd

I N THE PREVIOUS TWO CHAPTERS WE DEVELOPED AN UNDERSTANDING OF caring relationships and attitudes that brings us to the vital center of what the Christian tradition has always said about the meaning of human life on earth. First, we have been created to love God our Creator with all our being, and in so doing, to find our greatest delight in life. Second, we are called to love one another, ourselves, and the world with a love like God's own. To help us fulfill this high calling, our tradition offers us one particularly powerful, captivating, and inclusive image: we are to express our love toward others in a form of caring like that between shepherds and their flocks. In this chapter we will look at the breadth and depth of this image for understanding how every Christian is to express care to others in the name of Christ.

MAKING OUR CARING CHRISTIAN

As we explore the imagery of shepherding, we will appreciate the uniqueness of Christian acts of caring and what makes them different from the many kinds of caregiving readily available. The point of this discussion will not be to show that the Christian community's practice of care is superior to everybody else's. People help each other in all sorts of ways, and we should give thanks to God that this is so. Rather, we will seek what is distinctive about how Christians are to care for others. But this effort is important, too. It addresses one of our deepest needs as ministers to others, the need for a clear sense of identity, of who we are as we offer our limited gifts in gratitude for what God has done for us.

Without a confident sense of what it means to care for someone as an expression of our faith, our caring acts will become halting at best. We may cling for a while to the techniques our trainers impart to us and make ourselves believe that all is well with us and with those we are caring for. Deep down, though, our doubts will increase about what we are doing and why we are doing it. When the uncertainty about the effectiveness of our caring becomes too much for us, as inevitably it will, we may drop by the wayside, remembering our faltering attempts at ministry as one of the most devastatingly negative experiences of our lives. A sense of Christian identity, however, helps make our caring acts renewing to ourselves, transforming to their recipients, and pleasing to our Lord.

WHAT THE BIBLE SAYS ABOUT SHEPHERDING

Even the most casual glance at our sacred Scriptures makes clear the irresistible attraction that images of shepherding have held and continue to hold for faithful people everywhere. From a host of passages that we could consider in depth and with great profit, five seem especially relevant and illuminative. The first is from what may be the most familiar text in the Bible:

> The LORD is my shepherd; I shall not want. He maketh me to lie down in green pastures: he leadeth me beside the still waters. He restoreth my soul: he leadeth me in the paths of righteousness for his name's sake. Yea, though I walk through the valley of the shadow of death, I will fear no evil: for thou art with me; thy rod and thy staff they comfort me. (Psalm 23:1-4, KJV)

The language is breathtaking. In it, the images of shepherd and of being shepherded are deliberately extended to become nothing less than representations of God. Can it be that the Holy One of Israel, upon whom we are also told no mortal can look and live, wants to be our shepherd? Can we allow ourselves wholly, completely, and gratefully to rejoice that the Maker of all things and Redeemer of all human history chooses to relate to us like a mortal shepherd does to a tiny flock? Can we allow God to come this close to us? Can we allow ourselves to draw close enough to God to be shepherded? Surely no usage of shepherding imagery could be more extravagant than this psalmist's. Or more accurate!

Throughout its history ancient Israel prepared us well to receive a God whose holiness does not inhibit us from boldly declaring that God to be a shepherd to his people. The earliest Christian communities believed so.

The second biblical text that is especially worth considering comes from New Testament times and speaks beautifully of the Word of God incarnate as a shepherd:

> "I am the gate of the sheepfold .... Anyone who enters through me will be safe: he will go freely in and out and be sure of finding pasture .... I am the good shepherd ... who lays down his life for his sheep .... I know my own and my own know me .... There will be only one flock, and one shepherd." (from John 10, JB)

And even as a lamb:

> "The Lamb that was sacrificed is worthy to be given power, riches, wisdom, strength, honour, glory and blessing .... To the One who is sitting on the throne and to the lamb, be all praise, honour, glory and power, for ever and ever." (Revelation 5:12-13, JB)

The fourth text is a startling and powerful reminder of the awesome responsibilities of those chosen to be shepherds of God's people on earth and on God's behalf:

> Woe betide the shepherds who let the sheep of my flock scatter and be lost! says the LORD. Therefore these are the words of the LORD the God of Israel to the shepherds who attend my people: You have scattered and dispersed my flock. You have not watched over them; but I am watching you to punish you for your misdeeds, says the LORD. I myself shall gather the remnant of my sheep from all the lands to which I have dispersed them. I shall bring them back to their homes, and they shall be fruitful and increase. I shall appoint shepherds who will tend them, so that never again will they know fear or dismay or punishment. (Jeremiah 23:1-4, REB)

In Judaism and Christianity, this text has functioned as a frightening warning primarily to religious leaders—in Christian terms, to priests and pastors as leaders of congregations. It reminds the rest of us that we are tended, sometimes well and sometimes poorly, by people like us, who are divinely appointed to care for us as a shepherd cares for a flock—and as God cares for the world. Those so appointed carry a heavy burden of accountability to those in their charge and to the One who has placed them in their charge. Nothing could be worse for them than being found wanting in their shepherding when God's time of reckoning draws near. Does this text have anything to say to lay shepherds? Yes!

As important as it is for religious leaders to behave in certain ways toward those they lead, the manner of their caring is no different from that which governs any caring relationship in our communities of faith. Whoever may be caring for whomever, the Scriptures define caring in the same terms. All Christian caring seeks to convey in God's name the message of grace, love, reconciliation, and new creation in and through every act of care toward another. This means that a pastor, priest, or elder caring for a congregation through preaching, teaching, administering the sacraments, visiting, counseling, and praying will express the same kind of tender, solicitous, and sometimes goading care that every layperson does while conversing one on one with a brother or sister in need.

Nothing said here is intended to ignore or repudiate the fact that members of the clergy have distinctive responsibilities to bear in their congregations. But however different some of the activities of the clergy are from those of the laity, if we are to take our Scriptures seriously, the same spirit must govern both: enthusiasm for bearing witness by words, presence, and deeds to God's hopes and plans for those placed trustingly in our care. As the passage from Jeremiah especially makes plain, our enthusiasm is to be accompanied by a tender and an anxious concern that our caring not fail to be what God desires from us for the other.

The Scriptures will not allow us to get too far away from shepherding imagery in all Christian caring, whether of the clergy or of the whole people of God. The image of shepherd moves us at a deep, even unconscious level. It arouses within us associations to the warm, comforting nurture and to the challenging guidance we have received all our lives by loving people in our families, churches, neighborhoods, and communities. All of these people were and are shepherds to us. And even though at times we may resist being either another's shepherd or a member of someone else's sheepfold, we cannot fail to acknowledge how basic the image is to any distinctively Christian understanding of human existence in the world. In the words of the fifth scriptural passage:

> Know ye that the LORD he is God; it is he that hath made us, and
> not we ourselves; we are his people, and the sheep of his pasture.
> (Psalm 100:3, KJV)

IS CARING REALLY ABOUT TENDING SHEEP?

The ease with which our sacred Scriptures compare caring for people with tending sheep can be startling when we bring to mind what real shepherds in real fields do and why real sheep need them so much. Shepherds devote their lives to guiding flocks of easily distracted sheep over sometimes-treacherous terrain to safe places for grazing and resting that the sheep will never find for themselves. Along the way, they must constantly protect their flocks from the elements and from predators. In doing so, they expose themselves to danger, for sheep often act stubbornly and stupidly, blind to the obstacles that threaten them and to their need for constant care. Capable shepherds unhesitatingly wield the rod against enemies and the staff to support themselves on difficult climbs and to prod as well as gently gather their sheep.

Because these kinds of things characterize the work of real shepherds tending real flocks, we must exercise great care in the ways we compare their work with our ministering to others. As caregivers, we may be like shepherds in some respects. But we are not shepherds in any literal sense. First, the people for whom we care are not sheep! Second, the terrain of our shepherding has little to do with mountains and meadows, terraces and caves, deserts and oases. Rather it has to do with people's growth toward God and into a love of all that God has created. The end of this journey is our joyful flourishing through self-giving on the world's behalf. The process of getting there is through cooperation rather than coercion. Along the way, we and our care receivers seek God's will for our relationship and for our lives. A shepherding relationship between people is a relationship between someone in need and his or her servant. Good shepherds do not minister from a position of power, and they do not manipulate their care receivers into regarding themselves as weak, inept, and dependent.

Literally speaking, therefore, we are not shepherds. But much that we do in our caregiving is like shepherding. Like shepherds of sheep, we work hard to ensure that those we serve are adequately nourished. The kind of nourishment we seek for our care receivers is spiritual, the kind of nourishment that will help them to see, appreciate, and express their life and destiny in God:

> "You should work, not for this perishable food, but for the food that
> lasts, the food of eternal life." (John 6:27, REB)

Where are we to find this kind of sustenance? The answer to this question is close by:

> "This food the Son of Man will give you, for on him God the
> Father has set the seal of his authority.... . I am the bread of life.
> Whoever comes to me will never be hungry, and whoever believes
> in me will never be thirsty." (John 6:27,35, REB)

For Christians, the most immediate source of spiritual food is and always has been a Christ-centered community of faith sustained by worship, prayer, the Scriptures, loving nurture, and service to others. As shepherds, we must see to it that those to whom we minister know about such resources and avail themselves of them at every opportunity. This might mean that we take them to the places where the community of faith gathers and then back to their homes. Or it might mean that we patiently listen to our care receivers' stories of disaffection with the church until they rediscover on their own a deep need for the kind of fellowship this same church can offer. However the matter may be addressed in individual situations, it is essential that it be addressed. Participation in the life of a vital community of faith is essential for our journey toward a life of praise and thanksgiving to God and loving service in God's name.

Since we bear the principal responsibility for guiding our care receivers to these green pastures, we are likely to feel from time to time that tending others' souls is a responsibility that weighs continuously upon our hearts. We should feel this way! Shepherding is serious business, for pastors and for every lay shepherd in the congregation as well. But it also can be a delight. For what could be more fulfilling than standing side by side with our care receivers to enjoy together new experiences of God's grace, love, and empowerment?

EVERY CHRISTIAN CALLED TO BE A SHEPHERD
Caregivers in many Protestant traditions have used shepherding imagery in an especially problematic way by identifying ordained ministry in terms of this analogy alone. Frequently the leader of the congregation is called nothing other than pastor, from the Greek word poimen, which means "shepherd." An analogy intended to inform the dynamics of specific clergy responsibilities, caring for the flock, became the name for congregational leadership. And this is strange, since pastors do considerably more than tend the members of their flocks personally—they also preach, teach, preside at worship, organize, discipline, evangelize, and serve the wider community. But identifying the whole of ordained ministry as pastoral has served the indefensible purpose of making laypeople feel that they are excluded from pastoral care. Rather than affirming that all caring is like the tending of sheep, pastoral care devolves instead into what pastors alone do to nurture people.

In today's church and world, it lacks credibility to maintain that only a pastor, priest, elder, deacon, or rabbi can provide care that is genuinely pastoral. Laypeople are effective caregivers in their own right, particularly when clergy make the effort to equip them for such service. In smaller churches, the laity typically provide a great deal of the soul care their congregations offer people. In larger churches, competent clergy know that lay involvement is indispensable to an effective ministry of pastoral care to the whole congregation and beyond, if for no other reason than that the pastor cannot do everything by himself or herself. And so we must stop using the word pastoral to refer only to the work of a congregation's leader. Instead we must use it to refer to a particular kind of caring relationship and attitude, one that all Christians are called to cultivate toward others, with shepherding as its central image.

In a truly caring congregation, shepherding will have to do not only with the relation between that congregation and its pastor and between the congregation's members but also with the congregation's responsibility for the well being of all of God's creatures in the church and in the world. The responsibility of which Jesus once spoke, for "other sheep of mine, not belonging to this fold" (*John 10:16*, REB), is the principal responsibility of the church today. The image of shepherding is most fully understood when it expresses the relationship God intends between the church and all of humankind. Only when the church reaches beyond its own to serve the needs of all people everywhere will there be the "one flock, one shepherd" that our Lord envisioned.

SOME QUESTIONS TO THINK ABOUT

1. Who were your principal shepherds when you were growing up? As you think back, how adequate was the shepherding they provided you? How receptive were you at various times in your life to others' shepherding efforts on your behalf?
2. What are some ways in which caring for another is not like shepherding?
3. Can you recall a situation in which you offered care to another as an expression of your faith as a Christian? What did you do that you would regard as explicitly Christian? How were your efforts received?
4. How comfortable are you now with thinking of yourself as a shepherd to someone else?
5. What do you regard as the principal gifts and strengths God has given you that you can bring to another?

4. The Basics of Shepherding Relationships: Empathy

"He calls his own sheep by name, and leads them out. When he has brought them all out, he goes ahead of them and the sheep follow, because they know his voice." (John 10:3-4, REB)

You were like stray sheep, but now you have come back to the shepherd and guardian of your souls. (1 Peter 2:25, JB)

THE PURPOSE OF THE NEXT FIVE CHAPTERS IS TO EXPLORE THE FOUNDATIONS of shepherding relationships sponsored by Christian congregations. Though the subject here and throughout the book is the shepherding ministry of laypersons, it will help the discussion to follow if we begin with something that is especially important for pastors to know. Every pastor's authority to function as a pastor derives more from what she or he does to build it than it does from the church's power to confer it. Those to whom a pastor ministers decide whether they will let that person truly be their pastor, however thoroughly and officially ensconced he or she may be in a particular pastoral assignment. Their decisions will be positive only when their pastors make the effort to win their trust by showing themselves to be caring and competent witnesses to the gospel in all of the circumstances of life.

What is true for pastoral relationships holds true as well for all helping relationships in the Christian community. Everyone who ministers to another has the similar task of doing well those things that make for a relationship of mutual trust and confidence, the only kind of relationship in which one person's caring for another can be effective. In the pages to follow, we will consider what makes it possible for anyone to accept the kind of care that one person feels called to offer others.

Whether lay or professional, every caregiver's helping potential derives from some combination of relevant skills, understanding of human nature and behavior, and knowledge of and capacity to reflect on one's own personhood. The more effective a helper becomes, the more fully developed will be his or her abilities to communicate well as a person, to confront himself or herself honestly, to look compassionately upon the distresses and the dreams of another, and to utilize training responsibly. Even with all of these virtues in place, however, there remains something more basic still to the possibility of effective caring for others: a certain quality of relationship between a care provider and a care receiver.

MAKING A CARING RELATIONSHIP POSSIBLE

Unless we are able to establish a relationship of trust with our care receivers, we are not likely to be of much help to them, no matter how wise and skilled we may be. Whatever time may be required, therefore, to establish trust before doing anything else will be time well spent. Relationship building yields good results later. By contrast, hurrying the initial process of establishing the caring relationship will undermine otherwise capable caregiving.

What makes for interactions that are crucial to helping people often has been referred to as the basic or core conditions of helping relationships. The terminology can be misunderstood. For instance, is it being implied that people seeking help must meet certain "conditions"—i.e., that they must establish themselves as worthy or deserving of care? Must they be believers, or members of the church, or not in trouble with the law, or not engaged in practices that violate church teaching in some way? These are misunderstandings; capable helpers would never allow their ministering to be limited in advance by such narrowly circumscribed conditions.

In spite of the possibilities for misunderstanding, however, "condition" is still a useful term to apply to helping relationships. In most areas of human life, unless certain antecedent conditions are met, not only are things not likely to change for the better; they may not change at all. Patients are not likely to get all the help their doctors can provide them unless they take prescribed medications, adjust diet and physical regimen, avoid harmful foods and substances, and the like. Couples are not likely to grow in their intimacy unless they are willing to negotiate and compromise, to express their feelings openly, to respect each other's values and rights, and to deal constructively with frustration and anger. Parishioners are not likely to get much out of their church affiliation unless they are willing to put something of themselves into it—their prayers, presence, gifts, and service. Just as there are conditions that must be met for many kinds of relationships to flourish, helping relationships have their conditions too.

Reference to basic or to core conditions for effective helping relationships does not mean that if the stated conditions are fulfilled the relationship is bound to be successful. The conditions we will look at in the chapters to follow are the necessary conditions for the possibility of effective caregiving. That is, without them, a truly helping relationship cannot come about. But, as we will see, fulfilling them will not be sufficient to bring about effective caring. Not all who seek another's help are prepared and willing to accept the consequences for their lives of making good use of the help they receive.

In this and in the next four chapters we will concentrate on several conditions for establishing an effective caring relationship that are well known and widely discussed among mental health professionals. The list will be somewhat briefer than some in the literature, for we will focus attention on just those conditions that are the most important for building helping relationships in Christian contexts. We will consider them as the foundation for the shepherding ministry of the church. To this end, this and the following chapters will concentrate on five conditions: empathy, genuineness, respect, hopefulness, and affirmation of the other's strengths. We will then turn to the most important practical skills that a shepherd must learn and use with some degree of proficiency. But from the outset, we must be mindful that skill, however artfully employed, will be of little use unless we have already established a context of trust by honoring the basic conditions that make any helping relationship possible.

Of all the conditions making caring relationships possible, none has been discussed more extensively than empathy. So important is this condition to caregiving that many training programs for both professional and lay caregivers give the substantial bulk of their time to empathy training. Many treatment failures in counseling, psychotherapy, and pastoral care are failures on the part of the respective caregiver to communicate sufficient empathy to the client, patient, or parishioner. Because this is so, we cannot overemphasize the role of empathy in being genuinely helpful to another.

Sharing Another's Feelings

The word *empathy* suggests a capacity to know others' feelings and to feel them oneself, an acceptance of others with whatever feelings they exhibit, and an expression of the knowing and the feeling as a part of caring about and for them. For some people, such knowing, feeling, accepting, and expressing seem to come naturally. For others they come with greater difficulty and only after training and practice. However it is acquired, the capacity to empathize and the nonjudgmental sharing of empathy are essential for establishing an effective caring relationship. We are not likely to be of much help to people who feel that we neither understand nor feel what they feel about the things that are happening in their lives. Nor will we be of help if we fail to express our empathy in ways they can recognize, or if we fail to affirm them in their feelings, no matter how difficult we may find it to do so.

It is not easy to feel and communicate empathy evenhandedly in any and all situations. Sometimes we may be repulsed by what another is saying to us, and our immediate impulse is either to attack or withdraw:

> *She's never been anything but a tramp and never will be anything but a tramp—I ought to kick her out of my house and tell her to never come back.*

Other times, we may find ourselves getting bored or impatient with what a care receiver is saying or not saying to us, and for a time our feelings may not be with that person:

> *And when I came out of the grocery store I saw June drive out, so we had the best conversation! Did you know that her son made honor roll at State? Can you imagine that? In high school he was nothing but a dumb jock with all the cheerleaders following him around like he was a king. June's husband is a really good accountant—he's saved us buckets of money over the years. We are so blessed with so many good friends, and a wonderful home, and loving children ...*

By now this person's caregiver may feel inwardly like having a nervous breakdown. Nevertheless, one way to fail to communicate empathy is to allow ourselves to be put off by, or to tune out, the feelings that a care receiver wants to share with us.

Maintaining Appropriate Distance

Another way to hinder empathy is to try to absorb the other's feelings as if they were our own. When we do this, we will feel close to the other, but so much so that our efforts to be helpful will become compromised. We will become as frightened, angry, discouraged, or guilt-ridden as they are and therefore unable to focus on their feelings and situation. Most importantly, we will be unable to bring the kind of new perspective on things that only some measure of distance from a problematic situation can make possible. Often, what a distressed person needs especially is gentle encouragement to look at his or her circumstances from a little different angle of vision, in a new light, from a new point of view—to see the half-empty glass of water as half full. But if we become too wrapped up in others' plights by making their feelings our own, we cannot be an agent of their release from bondage.

Empathy involves accurate discernment of how another is feeling, and in this sense it is a feeling-with (em-pathos). But empathy that facilitates effective caring proceeds from an appropriate distance and with appropriate detachment—not so much that the other's distress does not affect us, and not so little that we become overwhelmed by and stuck in it. We will not be helpful to another if we refuse to let the other's situation matter to us:

Jerry: *I know I shouldn't feel this way toward my father-in-law. He's an old man, and it all happened a long time ago. But every time I think about what he did to my wife when she was a little girl I want to go over there and start screaming at him so hard that I never stop. I hate him! I hate him! I wish he were dead! I want to kill the ————— myself.*

Shepherd: *Your wife seems pretty normal to me. Why get so upset over something that goes back such a long way?*

But we will be equally unhelpful by allowing ourselves to feel another's pain as if it were fully ours. For instance, another shepherd might have responded to Jerry as follows:

Shepherd: *Just your telling me about this makes me so mad I see red. I feel like we both ought to go over there and make sure that man never forgets what he's done.*

What Jerry is dealing with—there can be little doubt that early incest is involved—can try the objectivity of even the most experienced shepherd. And because this will be so, it is all the more important that anyone shepherding Jerry have an opportunity to deal with his or own feelings appropriately, in ways we will discuss later. But these feelings must be held in some kind of check while ministering to Jerry, or the ministering will fail. One way of expressing empathy in this situation might be:

Shepherd: *You and your wife have been dealing with the consequences of these awful things your father-in-law did for a long time, and they've* *been terribly painful. No wonder you feel the rage you do.*

There's More to Empathy Than Just Feeling

The capacity to feel empathy is the capacity to take an interest in another's situation, to appreciate the range and nuance of the other's feelings in the situation, and to desire to understand both the situation and the feelings fully and caringly. Empathic regard is acknowledging and validating another's feelings and cherishing the other in the situations to which the feelings are the reaction and the response. It is listening and dwelling with the other, making oneself present and not merely there. Empathy helps us to affirm others as God has created them, no matter how they may be reacting in whatever situation, and to overcome our tendency to urge them to be different for the sake of our own comfort level.

Genuine empathy helps us never to take for granted our own intuitiveness when the feelings of others are involved. Empathy helps us to wait patiently for the further disclosures that can help us understand better what is going on in others' lives. In the waiting, we stay clear of false reassurances of how well we understand them. One of the most off-putting responses to the suffering of another can be the expression "I know how you feel." This is so even on those rare occasions when we might be right. It is not that we should never say such a thing; sometimes it can provide the kind of bulwark against isolation and loneliness that a distressed person may most need. But saying it too soon and too glibly, when the other's trust has yet to be established, will nullify the kind of care we intend to express.

EMPATHY AND WARMTH

Closely akin to the expression of empathy, in the minds of many mental health professionals and researchers, is the establishment of emotional warmth in the caregiving environment. I have difficulty with this notion, even though I am aware of how important a factor it can be in assessing effective care. Perhaps an illustration will make my difficulty clear. A few days before I began writing these paragraphs, a friend and I were enjoying lunch in one of our favorite restaurants. Two men came into the restaurant, promptly registered their feelings of discomfort over how hot they felt, and welcomed the manager's adjusting the dining room's thermostat downward. Ten minutes later, three other diners asked for more heat. Shortly after they were accommodated, still others called for more air conditioning. My friend expressed regret that we had not thought to bring sweaters to don and discard as these negotiations continued. I agreed with him wholeheartedly.

It may be that the notion of warmth is hard to pin down until we feel what the right amount of warmth is for ourselves. The problem with this view, though, is obvious. Our inner thermostats differ considerably. What may feel like a warm, nurturing interpersonal environment to one person may seem distressingly cool to someone else and like an emotional hothouse to still another. If we focus too much on projecting adequate warmth to others and on monitoring how warm they are to us, we will miss many opportunities to communicate what is far less subjective and far more cogent to effective caregiving. Our primary concern should be to express our interest in what another is feeling, our desire to understand what the feelings are about, and our commitment to remain present and accepting through whatever may come next. When these things come across between caregivers and care receivers, the helping relationship will feel warm enough.

SOME QUESTIONS TO THINK ABOUT

1. Some people live by the philosophy that we should take things as they come, without making a fuss about it. Others complain a lot about their lives but don't do much to change anything. Still others work hard to get to the bottom of why and how things happen in life. What do you think and feel about each of these approaches to life?
2. How would you characterize the difference between the qualities of empathy and sympathy?
3. Do that you think you might have a difficult time shepherding some people? Why? What might you do that could make you more available to such persons in shepherding situations?
4. Imagine that you are having a conversation with someone you care about and that you find yourself distracted, bored, or impatient. What would you do to tune in to that person?

5. The Basics of Shepherding Relationships: Genuineness

CONSISTENTLY, THE NEW TESTAMENT BEARS WITNESS TO JESUS AS ONE who spoke with authority. Both the word used and the witness it conveys remind us that Jesus' credibility to his hearers—even to those who rejected him—had to do with how well his words and deeds seemed to express honestly who he was as a person. The Jesus remembered lovingly in the Gospels brought his life under the sway of the principles he preached and taught as the norm for others. He did not say one thing and do another. In the end, his integrity cost him life. "Father, if it be your will, take this cup from me. Yet not my will but yours be done" (*Luke 22:42, REB*). But "beyond all doubt," the centurion said, "this man was innocent" (*Luke 23:47, REB*). Jesus' authoritativeness flowed from the godliness that was at the center of his being.

BEING GENUINE

We, too, are godly at the center of our beings, for we are made in the image of our Creator. However, much of what we say and do flows from self-centeredness rather than God-centeredness. Worse still, we tend to be dishonest with ourselves and with others about that selfhood. Instead of acknowledging and sharing ourselves openly and delighting in those who share themselves with us, we concentrate on making an impression, on keeping up an appearance. We work at putting on a show for people, primarily to cover up what we do not want them to discover about us. We are afraid that revealing what our self-centeredness has made of us would put them off. Jesus has shown us a better way.

As New Testament scholars have reminded us, we can make too much out of what the Gospels tell us about the inner being of Jesus. The fundamental problem for the apostolic witnesses was to overcome the scandal of a man who was proclaimed to be the Messiah but suffered the ignominy of crucifixion and an obscure burial. Nothing that was known about Jesus' character proved to be of help in working through this problem. The Gospels tell us that Jesus' undeserved suffering is a matter of what God intended, a part of the salvation that God intends for us. Only the triumphant claim that God had validated Jesus' life by raising him from the dead sufficed to put into perspective the necessity of the cross.

This much acknowledged, there remains something fetching about the New Testament's picture of Jesus, especially its details about the humanness of the one who was sent by God to be the "Shepherd and Bishop" of our souls (1 Peter 2:25, KJV). The one detail that is especially important for our discussion is the oft-repeated witness to Jesus' authoritative presence and to what made it so. It is captured well in the New Testament word exousia: from one's being. Jesus had an authoritative bearing because everything that he said and did flowed from the depths of his humanness and from the vital center of his sense of calling. Later dogmatic formulations spoke of Jesus as fully and truly human along with his being fully and truly God, and those formulations used highly technical philosophical terminology to spell this out in an intellectually credible way. The apostolic witness itself can be expressed in less forbidding terms: Jesus is genuinely God and one of us.

At least since the time of Carl Rogers, modern psychotherapy has remained untiring in its insistence on the importance of a therapist's genuineness for a positive outcome in therapy. Often Rogerians refer to genuineness as congruence, with the emphasis falling on the perceived inner connection between what a therapist says, does, and is. Whatever may be the preferred term, it designates inner confidence, self-assurance, and humility that allow a therapist to be comfortable with himself or herself. The therapist will resist hiding behind credentials, success, training, and techniques and will project instead a human as well as professional concern for the well being of those who come for help. In shepherding terms, being genuine involves offering ourselves as finite, fallible, and fallen creatures, redeemed by God's grace and love, called and equipped to help others in the name of the One who continues to work redemptively on their and our behalf.

Genuineness and Humility

This kind of genuineness is not possible without fully confronting all that our faith has to say about what is in and between us as human beings. Most especially, being genuine means acknowledging and coming to terms with the facts that

- we are not our own;
- we exist because God has created us;
- we are accountable to our Creator for the lives we live;
- we fall far short of what our Creator hopes and wills for us;
- we are constantly being renewed in our capacity to live as our Creator intends by a God whose mercy is unfailing; and
- we and those we seek to help share our condition and our possibilities.

Or, more simply, being genuine means being humble and being grateful.

Shepherding is humbling, in the sense that doing it well requires acknowledging and then letting go of every tendency to think more highly of our knowledge, insight, and skills than we have any right to think. It is humbling in the sense that it calls us to set aside our own concerns and priorities for the sake of what is in the best interest of another. It is humbling in the sense that it follows in the footsteps of the One who chose not to grasp too tightly his equality with God but instead emptied himself and became a servant to all (*Philippians 2:6-8*). And it is a humbling endeavor in the sense that it asks us to withhold whatever praises that may be due our efforts on behalf of others, in order that they may be given directly and joyfully to God.

> After all, what is Apollos? What is Paul? Simply God's agents in bringing you to faith. Each of us performed the task which the Lord assigned to him: I planted the seed, and Apollos watered it; but God made it grow. It is not the gardeners with their planting and watering who count, but God who makes it grow.... We are fellow-workers in God's service; and you are God's garden.
> (1 Corinthians 3:5-9, REB)

Genuineness and Gratitude

But if shepherding others arouses in us a renewed awareness of our lowly state before God, it also arouses within us a profound sense of gratitude— for all that our loving God has done for us, in spite of our inadequacies and sinfulness, for all the good that God continues to see in us even when we lose sight of it ourselves, for all that God calls us to share with others, and for the receptivity of others to being shepherded in the name of Jesus Christ. The opportunity to render care to another human being as an expression of our trust in the everlasting promises of God is truly something for which to be thankful. When we become thankful for it and humble in fulfilling it, we will achieve the genuineness in relating to our care receivers that they most seek in us.

Genuineness is more than our inner consistency, integrity, and wholeness—physical, mental, and affective. It is a matter of being transparent to the One in whom we live and move and have our being. Much of the uniqueness of shepherding, in contrast to therapy, can be attributed to shepherds' prayerful cultivation of their God-given capacity for openness to the transcendent dimension of human life and destiny—to what God is doing everywhere and to the difference it can make for everyone. Without a strong faith in this transcendent dimension and in the God who is its source and sustainer, something will remain lacking in the genuineness of those whose caregiving is offered in the context of a caring congregation.

SOME OBSTACLES TO OVERCOME

Several things can get in the way of expressing genuineness to those in our care. One is a spurious commitment to be the agent of another's wholeness. Inexperienced therapists sometimes fall victim to the seduction of medical models of healing and curing people, as if psychotherapy or marriage and family counseling were somehow like a set of surgical interventions to fix broken bones or remove tumors. And even experienced pastors sometimes develop their own messiah complexes, viewing themselves as Christ's chosen and indispensable emissaries to the troubled lives of their parishioners.

Another obstacle to being genuine is particularly troublesome to lay shepherds. They feel that they do not help people in the ways that pastors or counselors do and that they should do more for their care receivers than listening, expressing concern, being a steady presence, praying with people, and sharing their pain. As if these were not the heart of shepherding and as if they do not do more for many people than any other form of caring! Shepherding is not fixing, curing, or saving people. It is humble and grateful self-giving, in the confidence that God can and will do far more for hurting people than either they or we can imagine or think. Our openness to God's working, in another's life and in our own, is a bulwark against falling into the delusion that for caregiving to be effective, we will make it so.

Another impediment to genuineness that lay shepherds sometimes manifest is excessive preoccupation with doing things as we have been trained to do, no matter what. Put differently, the point is that having to do it right all the time is a sure way to let a training manual get between honest human interactions and to make our care receivers uncertain of who we are as persons. A common experience of lay shepherds is finding themselves in situations that their training manuals have not anticipated. What then? They must begin functioning on their own! Often, as many lay shepherds have said to me with a gleam in their eyes, these are the times when the work begins to get interesting. One especially conscientious shepherd made his peers laugh one evening when he said, "When everything else failed, all I could think of was just to be myself." Though his group was small, their applause was momentarily deafening.

Nothing in the previous paragraphs should be read to imply that there is anything wrong about doing everything in our power to be helpful to another and to use every resource that training and ongoing supervision can provide for the purpose of enhancing our helpfulness. The primary point is that too much of any good thing can be counterproductive to effective caring, because it can put up obstacles to the human dimension of a shepherding relationship. This point is applicable to a third obstacle to genuineness in our caring, on which this chapter will close.

This third block typically comes not from within ourselves but from our care receivers, and it becomes a serious block when we allow it to stay in place. Consider the following brief conversation:

Walt: *I've gotta tell you that I consider it a great honor that you're my lay shepherd. I sure hope I can measure up!*

Shepherd: *Wow! Before I begin to think I'm a really big deal, tell me a little more about the feelings you're having right now.*

Walt: *You are a big deal to me. You do so much around the church. You were a great troop leader when my son was in scouting. You just seem to me to be a guy who's got it all together. And you've got a great sense of humor. It's no wonder the pastor was so enthusiastic with me about assigning you to me.*

Shepherd: *Thanks, Walt, for all this good stuff. God has been good to me and my family, and we feel richly blessed.*

This shepherd will not find it easy to put aside his press notices and get close to Walt by opening himself humbly to the difficulties that he is about to lay out. It can be tempting for him to continue counting his own blessings, to begin contrasting them with Walt's lack of them, and to bask in Walt's undisguised but naive adulation. He might even begin to think that he is now qualified, by virtue of his own successes in life, to figure out how Walt can become as successful as he is:

Shepherd: *Well, Walt, there's no reason why you can't be blessed as I* *am. All you have to do is pray more than anyone else, work harder than anyone else, and God will give you the breaks you need. Count on it!*

Walt: *That's great to hear. It's just the thing I need to hear right now.*

More than likely Walt needs to hear something different from this, something that is more responsive to him and less self-congratulatory on the part of his caregiver. This shepherd's strengths can be a significant asset to Walt, as Walt works out his own sense of what God is asking of him. However, they can also be a hindrance to his entering fully into Walt's situation and pain. Our sense of specialness, though grounded in a lively faith in God's mercy and love, can be as much an impediment to communicating genuineness to another as a compulsion to cure and an obsession with rightness can be.

We began this chapter by bringing into focus an important aspect of Jesus' impact on those who heard him and came to know him during his all-too-brief ministry on earth. He was genuine in his being and bearing, and his genuineness set for all his followers an example in ministering to others. Following his example, however, does not require that any of us be the perfect human being that he was. We are too sinful for that, and God knows that we are. We can aspire, however, to become better persons than we now are, with God's help. And we can acknowledge our aspirations and our failures honestly, whenever it becomes appropriate to do so. The example we set by such honesty can go a long way toward building the kind of trust that makes a shepherding relationship possible and helpful.

SOME QUESTIONS TO THINK ABOUT

1. What would you most like other people to think about you? How important is it to you that they think this way? How hard do you work at cultivating the image you want others to have of you?
2. Are there many things about you that you don't want others to know? How hard do you work at keeping people from finding them out? What do you think might happen if they did find out some of these things?
3. When you are being yourself around others, what are you like? How comfortable are you with just being yourself?
4. How strongly would you rate yourself as a genuinely caring person?
5. How strongly would you rate your ability to express to others the care that you feel for them?

6. The Basics of Shepherding Relationships: Respect

ONE OF THE MOST STRIKING AND PAINFUL THINGS ABOUT LIFE IS THE NUMBER of encounters we have with angry people. Their stress levels are high, and their tolerance for frustration is low. For our unintended offenses, they crave retaliation rather than reconciliation. To them, we are at best inconveniences. At worst, we are their enemies. Sometimes we may feel that they are enemies to us as well.

What rude and hostile people lack is respect for others. They show concern, consideration, or appreciation for others' situations and feelings only when they believe it to be in their interest to do so. Any deference they might display to another is usually for the sake of gaining an edge. They esteem only themselves, and sometimes not even that. Paying respect is only a formality to them, and truly honoring someone is without precedent. Curiously, one of the most frequent complaints of disrespectful people is that others do not show them the respect that they think they deserve.

As difficult as it is to be around such people, they remind us dramatically of how important showing respect is in genuine relationships and of how deformed a relationship becomes when mutual respect goes out of it. Only grace can heal the sin-sick soul, but for grace to abound, there must first be respect, in people's attitudes and in the environment to which they contribute. When the attitudes and the environment are full of respect, genuine caring can begin. When there is respect-full-ness there can be real and lasting change. To be sure, in the case of society's most contemptuous persons, our respect cannot be for what such persons are now. But we can be respect-ful of what, by God's grace and power, these persons can become.

RESPECT, UNCONDITIONAL POSITIVE REGARD, AND FAITH

On the issue of respect, like that of genuineness, the influence of Carl Rogers continues to be felt across many schools of psychotherapy and pas-toral counseling. Much of what we understand by respect Rogers wrote about as "unconditional positive regard." Rogers saw the development and the communication of such regard as obligations every therapist must assume as a necessary condition for his or her work. And he assumed that it is possible for people to set aside whatever prejudices, animosities, and judgmentalism they might harbor toward others in order to treat them as persons capable of fulfilling their highest and noblest aspirations. The over-ly optimistic attitude that shaped Rogers's general view of human disposi-tions was powerfully manifest in his discussions of unconditional positive regard. Attractive as his attitude is at first glance, however, it is significantly at odds with one of the most important insights that our faith has to offer into the understanding of who we are and why we do the things we do.

From the standpoint of the Christian faith, hardly anything could be clearer about us than our blatant incapacity to look upon one another pos-itively and unconditionally. Although we were created otherwise, the sin-ful condition that we have brought about in ourselves is a cause and an expression of our strong and almost irreversible tendency to reserve positive regard only for some others, and even for them only conditionally. We tend to reserve our love only for those we like. We know that our Lord calls us to the better way for which we were created, the way of giving ourselves to the tasks of serving others in his name. And we know that in him there is power available to keep us on that way. Our faith also reminds us, howev-er, that the vestiges and wages of sin in each of us are too powerful for us to sustain a positive regard for others without any conditions, no matter how noble we may believe the ideal to be and no matter how strongly we may strive to fulfill it. In order to deal with this failing, we need God's grace and mercy constantly.

If unconditional positive regard is beyond our capability, however, respectfulness is not, particularly if it is centered in faith's full understand-ing of our condition as human beings. From the standpoint of faith, all human beings are unique creatures of God, with a sacred worth grounded in God's mindfulness of us. We bear the image and likeness of God our Creator deep within us, and we share a calling from God to live together in partnership for the care of the earth. We can learn to respect others because God has created in us the capacity to do so. This capacity is like all the others that make us resemble our Creator God: the capacities for reasoning, choosing, and being responsible for our choices, communicating, loving, and eliciting love from others. These capacities are indestructible and inextinguishable; however, we may misuse and distort them for the selfish purposes that reveal our deepest desire to be God ourselves. That God-likeness in each of us, however defaced it may be in our present condition, God's own Son died to restore. And God's great work of restoration and reconciliation continues.

The meaning of every life, when it is viewed with eyes of faith, is to be seen in reference to God's all-encompassing work of bringing the whole of creation, including human history, to its appointed end and fulfillment. Our task, whether as caregivers or care receivers, is to find our distinctive place in this God-ordained process. It can be profoundly liberating when as caregivers we discover that the respectful climate within which our work must take place requires for its sustenance far more than we can bring to the tasks and that the more is supplied each and every moment by the One who alone is our Healer, Sustainer, Guide, and Reconciler. God already respects the ones before us who challenge our capacities for respectfulness. But because God does, we are free to draw closer to them to discover the evidence, however obscured it may be, of divinely bestowed capacities in them whose activation can lead to a transformation in which God, too, can be well pleased.

RESPECT IS MORE THAN POLITENESS

Deep within each of us, as part of the divine image we bear, lies a capacity for respecting every human being and not just those who can do something for us. How do we strengthen that capacity so that it becomes a guiding principle for our lives? One answer to this question is to cultivate what we might call manners. As we will see, this answer is incomplete. Nevertheless, every culture has rules and rituals for expressing simple courtesy, for maintaining proper etiquette. Until recently, most cultures have made it a matter of importance that their young be schooled early in the art of conventional pleasantries and behaviors. One of the most poignant signs of the massive breakdown of civility is that fewer and fewer children and youth seem to grow up with much knowledge of how to be polite to others. Instead, a style of reach-grab-and-get-mad is becoming the order of the day. One important way of influencing and expressing respect for others is to honor anew our culture's rules for treating people with courtesy.

But more is involved in the process of becoming respectful of others than observing etiquette. Outward politeness often has little to do with the quality of a person's inner character. Niceness, for instance, can cover up selfishness, snobbishness, and manipulativeness. Nice people can be angry and calculating, using their carefully cultivated outward appearance to gain personal advantage, even at another's expense. This does not mean that there is no place for being outwardly courteous, polite, and nice when we would prefer not to be. Cultivating appearances can go a long way toward preventing the negative consequences of forgetting the niceties in dealing with people. But a mere outward show of courtesy will never be enough for a shepherding relationship to flower. The kind of respectfulness that every shepherd must strive to cultivate will require more than periodic checks of the right sections of manuals on etiquette. The more is nothing less than a sustained vision of what another person means in the sight of God, no matter what our assessment may be of what that person can mean to anyone else, ourselves included.

Learning Self-Respect

In two ways we can cultivate this deeper kind of respectfulness. One is to learn to respect ourselves more. Most of the negative attitudes that we carry around toward particular people root in still deeper negative attitudes about things in ourselves. We look down upon those who remind us of whatever we fear and do not want to look at in ourselves. Most prejudices do not arise from concrete encounters with those against whom we harbor the prejudices:

Jack: *I have every right to be mistrustful of the Koreans who are moving into this neighborhood. It was a Korean who drove my father out of business when I was growing up.*

Or:

Joan: *Now I know why I'm so mistrustful of men. My father ran off with another woman when my mother was pregnant with me, and she never got over it.*

While the form of these statements suggests that there might be something understandable about a person's disrespectful attitude toward one group or another, the reasons cited in them are hardly credible. Instead they cry out for further examination. Both statements collapse from the weight of false and faulty generalizations. What can a negative experience with one Korean family have to do with how anyone should look upon all

Koreans? And what can one irresponsible father have to do with how a woman should regard all men?

Both these statements reveal something far deeper in those who make them than their irrationality. In most cases, statements like these reveal powerful, underlying wishes to do to someone else what was done to them, coupled with mild to abject horror at that possibility. Jack wants to get even with Koreans. Joan wants nothing to do with men, except to punish them. The way they deal with their discomfort is by means of what psychologists call projection and what Jesus referred to as decrying the speck in another's eye while refusing to look at the log in one's own (*Matthew 7:3*). When we do not acknowledge and deal with what we do not respect in ourselves, we single out others whom we believe, sometimes rightly and sometimes wrongly, have similar dishonorable qualities and unload on them all the hostility that we otherwise would have to direct at ourselves. Scapegoating is another way of describing the process.

The way beyond such disrespect of others is to bring into view whatever we do not like about ourselves and to work on changing what may need changing, so that we will have a healthy self-respect. After all, Jesus' Great Commandment asks that we learn to love our neighbors as we love ourselves. In the work, we may find that what we do not like about ourselves is worthy of our respect and nurture—that we have been wrong about ourselves. Or we may find that what we do not like about ourselves is not worthy of our respect and nurture and therefore is something that, with God's help, we can and should change. In either case, the result should be that we no longer feel the need to find scapegoats and to force ourselves to see them in a negative light. Jack, for instance, allowed himself to see how strongly acquisitive he was and how he was willing to shove aside anybody that he felt was getting in his way:

Shepherd: *It's been hard to forget the person who caused your father so much trouble when you were growing up. I'm having a little difficulty, though, understanding why all Koreans must be like that one.*

Jack: *Whenever I see a Korean, I can't stop thinking back to that sneaky guy who opened up that big store next to Dad's and kept his prices so low that we couldn't compete.*

Shepherd: *You've had trouble turning off the memories of a bad time. It worries me a little that the memories may be getting in the way of your seeing what some other Koreans might really be like.*

Jack: *My mind's already made up—is that it?*

Shepherd: *Well, I guess it's just that I've come to see you as such a fair-minded kind of guy, and it's hard to figure you, when you go on the way you do about Koreans you haven't even met.*

Jack: *You're right. I wonder why I'm doing this to myself. Maybe it gets to me that we weren't able to keep up back then. Maybe I'm blaming that Korean for being better at business than my dad was.*

Shepherd: *You've described yourself as pretty competitive. Maybe you're more like that Korean than you ever thought you were.*

Jack: *That's a thought! And the truth of it is that I'm just as hard on my competitors as he was on Dad.*

Shepherd: *Is it OK with you that you're this way?*

Jack: *No, it's not a very Christian side of me.*

Shepherd: *Want to change it?*

Jack: *You know, I think I do.*

Jack's shepherd ministered to him effectively in this difficult situation. As did Joan's, who helped her to look deeper into herself and to acknowledge a childlike fantasy of a blessed union with her father, the one who abandoned her and her mother:

Shepherd: *Some of the feelings you're sharing seem to be about your father's running off from you, too.*

Joan: *I hadn't thought about it that way. All I remember was how depressed and angry my mother was for so long.*

Shepherd: *Did you feel that way, too?*

Joan: *Sometimes, I guess. Mostly, though, I just kept on wishing that he would be there. So many people in the family kept on saying so many good things about him.*

Shepherd: *It would have been nice to have all those good things wrapped up in a daddy all your own.*

Joan: *Maybe that's what I've been looking for in all the men I've gone with.*

Shepherd: *You've often said to me that the men in your life have all been huge disappointments.*

Joan: *Who could have measured up to my fantasies? I guess I'd better try to look at the next man who comes along a little more objectively.*

Respect and Gratitude

Another way of cultivating respectfulness is to focus our thoughts and meditations with greater regularity on the mercies that God has shown toward us. When Paul wrote to Timothy his especially well remembered words, "Christ Jesus came into the world to save sinners," he immediately and tellingly added: "and among them I stand first" (*1 Timothy 1:15*, REB). Then he praised God for his mercy and his "inexhaustible patience." This kind of spirit can make it possible for us to show respect to even the most disrespectful and disreputable among us.

The God who shows mercy to us, who is patient with us even as our sins abound, also and at the same time stands ready to be merciful to everyone else. The more aware we allow ourselves to be of God's respect for each and every one of his creatures and of the wideness in God's mercy, the better able we will be to sustain the respectfulness that is necessary for effective caregiving. Or, in language reminiscent of 1 John, we respect others because God has respected them first.

Respect is valuing the dignity and sacred worth of another person as God's creation, who by God's grace has his or her own role to play in the great drama of the redemption of all creation. However displeasing other persons' feelings, thoughts, decisions, and actions may be to us, if we are to accomplish anything as their shepherds, we will have to find a way to set our displeasure to the side and begin the arduous process of winning their trust. This does not mean that we are under an obligation to feel the way they feel about things, to agree with their thinking or their decisions, or to affirm every action they take. It does mean, however, that we must have regard for and take protective care of their rights as human beings and of their identity as children of God. It may be useful in the process to acknowledge that their problems, dysfunctionality, slowness to learn from their mistakes, resistance, or waywardness may differ only in degree from our own.

SOME QUESTIONS TO THINK ABOUT
1. In your circle of acquaintances, is there anyone you try to avoid or especially dislike? What about him or her seems to set you off?
2. Does the person you described remind you of anybody else you have known in your life? What was your relationship with that person like?
3. Probably you think of yourself as quite different from the people you have described. Try to describe some things that you share with them (e.g., blue eyes? being overweight or underweight? coming from a dysfunctional family? being divorced? an interest in sports?)
4. Think about a time when you found yourself offering care to someone whom you did not like. How did you deal with your feelings of dislike while you also provided the care called for?
5. Do you believe that there are people whom God does not love? What to you are such people like? Could there be any hope for them?

7. The Basics of Shepherding Relationships: Hope

Now faith is the substance of things hoped for, the evidence of things not seen. (Hebrews 11:1, KJV)

ONE OF THE MOST FAMOUS AND WELL-LOVED PASSAGES OF THE NEW Testament, Hebrews 11:1 is nevertheless notoriously difficult to translate. The proliferation of new versions of the Bible seems almost to give us different messages about the verse's central theme, the relationship between faith and hope. In the paragraphs that follow, I have gone back to the easy familiarity of the King James Version. So rendered, the text in Hebrews has considerable bearing on maintaining effective shepherding relationships, as well as pastoral and therapeutic ones.

HOPE MAKES THE DIFFERENCE

Many researchers, attempting to determine whether some kinds of psychotherapy yield predictably better outcomes than others, have made an important observation about the power of hope in therapy, regardless of the kind of therapy in which hope is communicated. I will state the observation in a more dramatic way than researchers tend to be noted for, but in a way faithful to their conclusion. What seems to make psychotherapy work, especially in many difficult kinds of long-term cases, is not the faithful application of the premises and the techniques of any particular school but rather the therapist's unshakable conviction that things can and will turn for the better. The effective therapist refuses to give up and never loses hope.

This is so in the ministry of shepherding as well. Without a tenacious holding onto hope, even in the most dismal of circumstances, lay shepherds may not be able to help others to adjust to their circumstances, to grow in their faith, or to make the changes not only to improve their lives but also to become the persons God calls them to become. As the verse from Hebrews might be paraphrased: without hope, faith, lacking substance, is dead.

In shepherding relationships, hope is fundamentally an anticipation of positive change in external circumstances, and more importantly, in the inward processes of responding to them. One of the most important tasks that any shepherd can undertake is seeing that hope prevails, especially for those who believe that their lives will never get better. Sometimes what our care receivers most need to see in us is an unassailable conviction that most obstacles to their making changes in themselves are surmountable with God's help.

Hope and Realism

But hopeful caregivers also know that changes for the better often do not look like such. For instance, a woman who is being destroyed by an addiction to harmful substances may have to undergo an excruciatingly painful period of detoxification and withdrawal in order for her life to get better. It will not be helpful to offer this woman the false assurances that distressed family members and friends sometimes fall back on, such as

> There's nothing to worry about. Giving up that awful stuff will be a lot easier than you think.

Or

> The treatment you have to go through will be over before you know it, and then you'll be happier than you've ever been in your life.

Further, many of the changes that people wish for may not be possible. A man who leaves his wife for someone else may never come back, no matter how strong that wife's wish may be that someday he will return. The following examples of statements in this kind of situation, though probably motivated by sincere concern, reinforce denial and illusion:

> Shirley, I know that Jim loves you very deeply and that this other woman can't hold a candle to you. One of these days he's going to wake up and come crawling back to you.

> All men are like this sometimes, Shirl. You keep your spirits up and everything will work out for the two of you.

Whenever we find ourselves working with someone on something that any reasonable outside observer would regard as hopeless, one of the things that ought to occur to us is that our persistence may be grounded in nothing but fantasy. Maybe we, too, naively wish that things will get better. For instance, even a well-meaning prayer for a miracle, offered by a shepherd whose personal faith is beyond dispute, can distract desperate care receivers from giving themselves over to what can be hoped for (e.g., a peaceful death rather than a protracted, agonized grasping for a cure that is not to be) and keep them mired in an unreality that will defeat them. There is a profound difference between hoping and wishing, between inviting people to realistic anticipation and encouraging them in a fantasy.

Hopeful and effective shepherds hope realistically. But they also trust steadfastly that in any and all distressing situations, there are always things to be hopeful about, and that focusing on those things is often the best way to resolve the distress. In the following paragraphs, we will explore the question of the source of such hope and the ways in which the true source of hopefulness lies somewhere else than in our capacity to dwell delightedly in comforting images of our own making.

WHAT MAKES HOPE POSSIBLE

To begin, let us acknowledge immediately that to some extent most of us can cultivate a sense of hopefulness whether or not we are hopeful by nature. We can always work on developing a positive mental attitude. Telling ourselves often enough that a glass of water in front of us is half full rather than half empty may bring about at least a modest alteration in what we see. And practicing optimism might make it easier for us to smile encouragingly at those in our care. In these senses, hope can be learned, just as other techniques for enhancing our caregiving can be learned, practiced, and made increasingly more effective. But the question remains: Are we learning to be more hopeful in these processes, or are we only acquiring sophistication in appearing more hopeful? False bravery in the face of serious setbacks, forced smiles in response to deep disappointments, refusal to let anything get to us—these are not ways of engendering genuine hope.

It does not help us much, therefore, to think of hope as something like a developed skill that we can practice to perfection. Instead, hopefulness is more like a basic outlook or attitude that shapes who we are and how we look at everything in our experience. Hope's growth in us has less to do with our being intentional and rigorous about its cultivation than it does with our deepening understanding of human nature and possibilities, along with the foibles to which human beings are heir. Part of this understanding takes the form of a practical wisdom that can come only from personally facing enough of life's setbacks, living through them, and taking satisfaction from surviving them. Enduring and prevailing over illness, disease, abuse, pain, disappointment, loss, neglect, and our bad choices can make hope more plausible. As most participants in recovery groups know well, there is something uplifting about hearing consistently from those who are out ahead in the recovery process, "I am making it, and you can, too."

At a deeper level, the kind of understanding from which hope springs is theoretical more than practical in nature. It is characterized by *theoria*, a certain way of seeing things whole. Specifically, it is an understanding influenced by vision. It takes the form of a comprehensive perspective on the origin, nature, and destiny of human beings. Rightly grounded, a vision about what human beings are like and what is possible for them can convince us on rational grounds to point our expectations in a hopeful direction. The more we work with such a theory, applying it over time to a greater and greater variety of circumstances, the stronger our sense of hope can become.

However, just as the right vision can stimulate our capacity to hope, the wrong one can undermine that capacity. For instance, Freudian determinism, in showing us how to become insightfully resigned to the inevitable, trains adaptiveness at the expense of our yearning for the unprecedented. Many other modern-day psychotherapies seem to be able only to leave us with the cold comfort that life will consist of what we can do to make it meaningful for ourselves, sometimes but not always with the help of others.

Consistent application of a holistic perspective on human existence can contribute a great deal to our becoming more hopeful about the outcomes of our caring ministry, and only a right vision can do this. Vision, however, is not the source of hope but its nurturer. It may be that the choice of a vision—or a theory—upon which to rely is a function of the degree of hopefulness that is or is not already within us. We become loyal to the vision or theory that is as hopeful or as hopeless as we already are. From this perspective, hope begins to look more like what the ancient Greeks called an excellence of character and what we often refer to as a virtue. We bring to our vision-making and our theorizing something deep within us, and deeply true about us, and for its sake we develop the outlooks that we do. The analogy between hope and the virtues is helpful as long as we do not suppose that the only source of character excellence is human beings and that we alone are responsible for the virtue that we enjoy. Instead, Paul writes of hope as one of the gifts of the Spirit.

HOPE, VISION, AND FAITH

The applicability of Hebrews 11:1 is now evident. Only one understanding of the human condition can provide an adequate rational ground for hopefulness. Not our own inferences but rather God's gracious working within and between us forms this understanding. It is embedded in God's gift to us of the capacity to trust the Lord with our whole being and of activating that capacity by means of the life, ministry, death, and resurrection of his only Son. Our source of hope is not vision focused through the lenses of modern philosophy or psychology. Rather, we attain to the fullness of hope through sustained and grateful reflection on the divine act of grace that is the beginning of faith. What gives substance to our hope is faith; faith and not scientific, philosophical, or psychological theories "convinces us of realities that we do not see" (REB). Or, faith alone "can guarantee the blessing that we hope for, or prove the existence of the realities that at present remain unseen" (JB).

If hope's wellspring is faith, and if hopefulness grows in us as we reflect continuously on that faith, what will be the content of our hope? For Paul, it is the unconquerable assurance that all things are being brought to their perfection by the God who created them and that as a consequence, all our caregiving in the name of Jesus Christ participates in a process of divine transformation of the whole of creation:

> For I am persuaded, that neither death, nor life, nor angels, nor principalities, nor powers, nor things present, nor things to come, nor height, nor depth, nor any other creature, shall be able to separate us from the love of God, which is in Christ Jesus our Lord. (Romans 8:38-39, KJV)

The author of 1 Peter frames the Christian hope more in terms of a life beyond whatever transformation God may effect throughout the created universe. At 1:3-4 (REB), he writes:

> Praised be the God and Father of our Lord Jesus Christ! In his great mercy by the resurrection of Jesus Christ from the dead, he gave us new birth into a living hope, the hope of an inheritance, reserved in heaven for you, which nothing can destroy or spoil or wither.

The reference to the resurrection seems to function as something of an answer to an implied question that comes later in the letter, a question that has been the overarching concern of this chapter: What is the basis for hoping as we believe we must hope in order to be genuinely helpful in our ministry? The writer makes reference to this question in terms of our responsibility to give an account of our hope: "hold Christ in your hearts in reverence as Lord. Always be ready to make your defense when anyone challenges you to justify the hope that is within you" (*1 Peter 3:15, REB*). For him, as for Paul, the defense of our hope—whether our hope is for transformation in this life, for blessedness in the next, or for both—is our faith that Jesus Christ was raised from the dead by God and that as he now lives, so, too, shall we live.

This stratum of the New Testament raises an interesting and possibly an unnerving question: Unless we can affirm Jesus' resurrection from the dead, do we have any grounds for being hopeful? Poignantly, Paul writes to the Corinthians: "If it is for this life only that Christ has given us hope, we of all people are most to be pitied" (*1 Corinthians 15:19, REB*). While many Christians have found a basis for hoping in other parts of the Christian message as well as this one, what Paul and all the great cloud of witnesses call us to confront is that we must find somewhere in the message of Christ's triumph over death the ground for our hopefulness, or else what we do strive to hope for will be without any secure foundation.

What do we learn from our faith about hope? First, it is a gift far more than it is an achievement, a gift whose ultimate source is God. Second, it is alive in us already, we do not have to create it. Third, it is connected in the closest possible way with the Christian community's jubilant witness at all times and everywhere to the ever-living Christ. And finally, its content has to do not only with the time and history that like an ever-rolling stream eventually bears all its sons and daughters away, but also with what is heavenly. To live in hope is to live toward something that nothing on earth can ever take away:

> *I foresaw that the Lord would be with me forever,*
> *with him at my right hand I cannot be shaken;*
> *therefore my heart is glad*
> *and my tongue rejoices;*
> *moreover, my flesh shall dwell in hope,*
> *for you will not abandon me to death,*
> *nor let your faithful servant suffer corruption.*
> *You have shown me the paths of life;*
> *your presence will fill me with joy.* (Acts 2:25-28, REB)

The defense, then, for our hopefulness as others' shepherds is and must remain anchored in our faith. In this faith orientation, among the many models of healing, Christian caring finds its uniqueness.

SOME QUESTIONS TO THINK ABOUT

1. In times when you found it hard to be hopeful, what kept you going?

2. What do you understand to be the principal differences between realistic and unrealistic hope?

3. Do you believe that there is always something to be hopeful about, whatever our circumstances may be? If you do, what has contributed most to your coming to this conviction? If you don't, how would you help someone who seems genuinely hopeless about life?

4. What are your most fundamental convictions about the nature and destiny of human beings?

8. The Basics of Shepherding Relationships: Affirmation

MOST COMPETENT THERAPISTS KNOW THAT MANY IF NOT MOST OF THE positive results from any course of psychotherapy can be attributed not to their work but rather to what the client or patient chooses to do for himself or herself in and following the therapy. Some researchers claim to have established that 40 percent of therapy outcomes can be accounted for in this way. Whether this striking figure is proven or not, most experienced practitioners would have no difficulty affirming that care receivers play the decisive role in the effectiveness of most of the care they are offered. Perhaps the 40 percent figure is too low, especially with respect to lay caregivers! My own sense is that 80 to 90 percent of the latter's effectiveness lies with their empathy, genuineness, respectfulness, and hopefulness.

HELPING PEOPLE TO HELP THEMSELVES

The major source for positive change in the people to whom we minister—whether we are professional therapists, pastors, or lay shepherds—is more in them than in us. And it rests in God more than in all of us together. What does this mean for our shepherding? Principally it means that if we are to be effective, we must involve those to whom we minister in their own growth and in solving their own problems—with their God-given capacities, in the light of their faith, and by constantly attuning their wills to God's will. We are to take our satisfactions more from what they do than from what we may do to be of help. Sometimes this proves difficult, especially when we fall into doing for our care receivers because we assume that they cannot do for themselves without close, constant watching from us. What family therapists refer to as overfunctioning occurs also in shepherding, and it is cured, if at all and paradoxically, only by a shepherd's learning to work hard at not working so hard. Things go even better when shepherds work harder to identify and affirm the other's strengths than to take pride in their own.

While we may not be able to determine precisely how much those who seek another's help are responsible for alleviating their own symptoms and for their own growth, the research cited above can offer some intriguing clues. For example, people who suffer from anxiety and depression may benefit as much from self-help approaches as they do from strategies coordinated by professionals. This is not to say that self-help groups will help everyone so suffering or that professional treatment should never be recommended.

Another interesting research finding—or a seriously entertained hypothesis—is that we may not be able to establish clear, positive correlations between the effectiveness of treatment in general and therapists' level of training and experience. Younger, less experienced, and less well trained therapists appear to do about as well as seasoned veterans do in caring for people. Further, no particular kind of therapy seems to be more effective than any other, across the whole spectrum of human problems. The positive correlations with good outcomes in therapy appear to be of a different sort. What counts especially is the personhood of the therapist and patients' willingness to help themselves.

If helping people to help themselves is a major goal of practically all forms of psychotherapy, then it should be a goal of the shepherding of souls as well. Empathy, genuineness, respect, and hopefulness can establish effective caring relationships that reduce significantly the difference between lay and professional caregivers, pastors included. We can now add that the care provider's commitment to help others to discern their unique abilities, interests and goals and to deepen in their relationship with God is of singular importance for realizing the full potential of caring relationships. In the Christian community, though, helping people to help themselves cannot refer to any single strategy applied unthinkingly to anyone and everyone requesting care. Why is this so?

WHO WANTS TO BE HELPED?

One way to answer this question is to refer to the makeup of the typical congregation. In it are four groups of people who contribute significantly to shaping the total context and the varying strategies of shepherding ministries. In the first group are those who cannot care for themselves and who must depend on others if their basic human needs are to be met. This group includes especially very young children, infirmed older people, and the seriously ill and disabled. It makes no sense to insist that shepherding such persons must focus on discerning and affirming their strengths. Rather, responsible shepherding must include doing everything possible to ensure their safety, prevent further harm to them, and build and maintain a structure for consistent, high-quality caring that provides what persons in this group cannot provide for themselves.

In the second group are people who accept care when they need it, who give care unhesitatingly when others need it, and who are grateful to receive from and to give to others. Because these people already know something of their God-given capacities and of the interdependency of the human condition, they are likely to be the strongest resources in congregations' ministry of shepherding. As such, they call for a relatively simple strategy: Put them in caregiving roles as much as possible and affirm them as congregational role models.

With people in these two groups, it is not difficult to work out the balance between helping people who cannot help themselves and helping people to help themselves and others. Shepherding becomes considerably more complex with persons in the third and fourth groups. The third is composed of people who refuse either to receive help from or to give help to others. Their credo is God helps those who help themselves. They save some of their most caustic criticisms for the poor and the homeless and announce with certitude that only those who fail to make use of the many (equal) opportunities our society generously holds out to everyone need wind up needy. Every parish and every community has its share of self-righteous folks whose God is the rules they have rigorously set and kept, all the while relying on no one to give them anything for nothing.

We are not likely to be of much help to people in this third group by focusing our energies on helping them to discern and affirm their strengths. They are already too comfortable with what they think are their strengths. Because they do not allow themselves even passing awareness of their own vulnerabilities, they are unable to appreciate anything that remotely looks like vulnerability, weakness, or dependency in others. Most parishioners like this sorely try the patience of their pastors and sometimes drive them to a similar kind of judgmentalism. No longer willing to let unfeeling criticisms of the truly needy go unchallenged, pastors may throw caution to the winds, mount their pulpits with a moral indignation worthy of the most raucous of the Old Testament prophets, sound loudly the liberationists' affirmation of God's preferring the poor, the weak, and the needy of the world, and wait boldly for the conversions that never seem to come. In their rush to afflict the comfortable, such pastors lose the discernment that this kind of comfortableness has a disturbingly defensive quality about it and that below its surface is the fear that life may turn out to be unmanageable, even for those who have spent most of their lives denying that this could be so.

The comfortable are already afflicted, therefore. They need what many of their pastors and fellow laypersons often run out of: patience. Out-of-sorts pastors and laity will not succeed in their efforts to substitute thundering denunciation for subtle, persistent guiding of their too assured parishioners toward those kinds of interactions that alone have the power to soften and to change hearts. We cannot overemphasize the importance of ensuring that parishioners who think they know what human beings are like have ample opportunities to reevaluate their suppositions through constant contact with and ministering with those who are most unlike them—those they especially do not like and respect.

Initially most such contacts serve only to confirm self-righteous persons' most ardent suspicions that out there are all sorts of lazy, indifferent, manipulative, and untrustworthy folks interested only in getting more for themselves than they deserve at the expense of honest, hardworking people too gullible for anybody's good. But if the contacts come frequently enough and with sufficient variety, and if they are talked about and reflected on openly, there is a good chance that some of them will begin to break into the hard-heartedness and closed-mindedness of the condescending and initiate a process that can be genuinely transforming. If there are no guarantees that this will happen, there is also certainty that without enhancing comfortable people's social awareness, nothing else will prove effective either.

The fourth group typical in congregations and the communities to whom they minister is composed of people who wrongly assume that they cannot take responsibility for their lives and that, accordingly and equally wrongly, they must get others to take care of them. When they succeed in securing another's help, they remain grateful until their demands escalate beyond the other's willingness and ability to meet them. When they fail to convince someone else to take care of them, they get angry. Their frustrations, unhappiness, and misery are to them always someone else's fault. And because they choose not to see themselves as capable of protecting and defending themselves, they ferret out blame to affix to anyone but themselves. Their sense of helplessness is carefully taught and quickly caught. It is accompanied by an exquisitely cultivated petulance: "I can't"; "I won't"; "Try to make me."

Nothing in the previous paragraph should be construed as minimizing the reality, scope, and severity of oppression, neglect, victimization, abuse, and dehumanization that are prevalent in the human community—and have been from the beginning. For many, the impact of such processes includes rendering them, temporarily and in some cases permanently, incapacitated. These are people whom we properly regard as members of the first group cited above. Here, however, we are referring not to the genuinely victimized but to those who have taken up a posture of a victim and who have chosen to make that posture synonymous with their being and personal identity: they are nothing but victims. They make a calling out of remaining helpless and hopeless dependents, even though they are more than capable of taking responsibility for their own lives and of becoming more caring of others. Effective shepherding of people who like to play victim will require from us a strong willingness to hold them accountable for their negativity.

HOLDING PEOPLE ACCOUNTABLE

The first approach is to hold people accountable for the gifts God has given them and for resisting every temptation to use their gifts first for their benefit or at the expense of others. As Christians, we believe that we find our lives by losing them for the sake of Christ and the gospel. This truth requires from our shepherding a steadfast confronting of people's carefully cultivated efforts to avoid, evade, deny, and repudiate the responsibility God intends that all of us assume for ourselves and for the well being of others. Psychotherapy typically conceives this approach in terms of holding people accountable for knowing what they want for themselves out of life and for exploring the realistic means available to them for achieving it. For faith, the issue is not so much knowing what we want from life as it is discerning what God calls us to do with it. In both cases, however, it is only self-deception to claim that taking responsibility for our lives is beyond our capacity.

Self-deception of this sort runs deep, however, and overcoming it often requires a second approach: the exploration of longstanding patterns of learned helplessness. The inertia to be overcome, in order to take charge of one's life and to use it well in the service of God's coming kingdom, draws much of its power from its rootedness in the coping strategies of whole families, often from generation to generation. So habitual are many of these strategies that few family members may be able to consider the possibility that things might be done differently and that, if they were, everyone might be better for it. The notion that we can't be whole on our own, that someone else must do for us, is as pernicious and contagious as it is destructive. Against it, the only effective inoculation is action based on insight into the peculiar forces within each family that maintains the notions at infectious levels. We need to learn with our care receivers how at least some in each family and in each generation keep themselves relatively free of the toxic effects that these forces have on the others. We can do this by talking with our care receivers about how things were done in their families when they were growing up, and how things might be different in present-day relationships. Most shepherds likely will have a story or two of their own to share!

A great deal of the help that comes in a shepherding relationship comes from the person being helped. Being truly helpful to another must include assisting the other to discover, claim, and make use of his and her insights, abilities, experiences, and faith—in order to resolve whatever brought that person to seek another's help. As we have seen, however, helping others to help themselves is more complicated than it might seem, because the principle does not apply to everyone in the same way. As there are four kinds of people who characteristically make up the membership of congregations, we must develop different strategies for accomplishing the goal that respects the characteristics people exhibit in each of these groups. How we affirm others' strengths will depend in large measure on who the others are, just as how the exercise of access, initiative, response, support, and confrontation in every shepherding situation will depend on the situation and on who happens to be caught up in it.

A REVIEW OF THE BASICS

From the perspective of our common faith, effective caring, whether in times of great distress or high aspiration, requires patient, compassionate reaching out and understanding. Such caring is offered by people who have an appropriate balance of confidence and humility and who are committed to nurturing in themselves the greatest helping skills of which they are capable. When caring takes the form of shepherding, what will be additionally in evidence is a caregiver's lively sense of gratitude to God and earnest desire to serve others in God's sheepfold as a witness of faith. Faith, eagerness to be of help, and relevant skills all are especially necessary at the beginning of a helping relationship, for without them it will be close to impossible to build the kind of trusting relationship that makes caring intentions and actions helpful. Trust building, by communicating empathy, genuineness, respect, hope, and affirmation of the other's strengths, is the most important thing any shepherd may accomplish in any caring relationship. In many caring relationships, this may be and often is enough.

SOME QUESTIONS TO THINK ABOUT

1. What have been your most significant experiences of caring for someone who cannot care for herself or himself? What feelings did you find in yourself during your caregiving? How effective do you think your caregiving was (is) in the situation(s)?

2. How easy or difficult is it for you to accept care from someone else?

3. What kinds of people do you think are likely to try your patience the most if you were to take on shepherding responsibilities to them? How might you deal with those frustrations when they arise?

4. When you want to rely on others more than you think you should, what gets you up and gets you going on your own?

9. Well Begun Is More Than Half Done

To this point we have looked at the foundations of caring relationships from the perspective of faith. Our discussions centered on the biblical image of shepherding and explored what a caregiver must be able to express in order to become another person's trusted shepherd. Underlying everything is the fundamental affirmation of our faith that God is calling all of us, whether we are clergy or laypersons, to be shepherds to one another and to all who are in need. But how are we to follow our calling specifically? What are we as Christian shepherds to do when we minister caringly to others? This chapter and the ones that follow will provide useful answers to these two practical questions. We begin with a discussion of how to start a shepherding relationship.

MAKING A CONNECTION

A young couple sat dejectedly in their pastor's office, pouring out their anger and despair over the impending collapse of their marriage. Wisely, the pastor determined that the couple's problems went beyond his range of experience and competence. He asked the couple whether they would be willing to give a professional marriage counselor an opportunity to help them put things back together. Somewhat fearfully, they agreed. Two weeks later, they called the pastor to tell him that they had proceeded immediately to make an appointment with the counselor he suggested and that their first two sessions went well.

During this time, another parishioner told this pastor that her grief over her husband's death was more than she could bear by herself and that she was going to see a psychiatrist the next day. She asked that the pastor say a prayer with her that she would get the help she needed from the therapist. After the next Sunday's service, the pastor quietly asked his parishioner, "How did it go Thursday?" She responded tearfully, "Terribly. I'm not going back. But there's another therapist in his building I've heard good things about."

These two vignettes tell us a lot about how people who struggle with problems in their personal lives typically go about getting the help they need: they reach out to someone they are willing to trust. If that person proves unable to help, they go to someone else. When people admit to themselves that they need help and acknowledge that they deserve it, their willingness to be helped often makes the difference in their getting the most out of the help that they eventually find. In short, people who need help typically take the initiative in establishing contact with the one they are willing to believe can and will help them.

The vignettes also reveal how professional care providers enter into relationships with people asking for their help. They communicate their availability, willingness, and competence, wait for someone to contact them, and then respond by doing everything within their power to establish trust quickly. All therapists hope that they will inspire a potential client to believe that their work together will prove beneficial. The best therapists seem to be able to accomplish this almost all the time. But even they have to admit that once in a while they are not able to reach some potential patients, no matter how hard they try. Setting aside the obvious fact that inept care providers rarely establish much contact, it is still difficult to predict whether there will be a good fit between a potential care recipient and even the most capable provider. I often think that the necessary connection between people is a matter of mystery rather than of happenstance. In the first instance above, therapist and client connected; in the second, they did not. And we may never know for sure why one pairing worked and the other did not.

HELPING REQUIRES CONNECTING

We can be sure that no caregiving will occur without genuine contact and connection. Someone in need must be ready to receive a caregiver's efforts on his or her behalf. The caregiver must be ready and competent to render the care needed. And the two must see in each other enough that they can trust in order to allow the relationship to begin. The caregiver bears the greater responsibility for contact and connection. Would-be caregivers must give whatever time and energy it takes to build a care receiver's trust. None of the other techniques for rendering care prove of any benefit without trust. Hard work expended at the beginning to establish the basic conditions of an effective relationship—conditions we have looked at previously—usually (although not always, as the second vignette suggested) produces rich dividends, encouraging the care receiver to entrust more and more of his or her struggles and dreams to the one reaching out in love to be of help.

As the discussion to this point has shown, it is not difficult to describe the usual way that people get needed care from a family member, friend, or professional caregiver: they approach the other directly. The process is somewhat different, however, for most caring relationships that involve lay shepherds. Here, contact presupposes that someone else has already made a referral. The process usually involves something like the following.

A pastor, another church staff member, or a lay coordinator of the congregation's shepherding ministries intervenes on behalf of another. The person may be in crisis, or in a struggle with moral or faith questions, or in a major growth phase in his or her life. Care appropriate to the immediate situation is rendered, but follow-up is needed. The problem is that the pastor or other caregiver usually must go on to other crises and other requests for help. This is the entry point for most effective ministries of lay shepherding. The first caregiver raises with a person needing longer-term ministry the possibility of receiving into his or her life a lay shepherd who can meet with the person on a one-to-one basis for as long as it takes. A typical conversation might proceed as follows.

Care Receiver: *Every time I let myself think that I'm beginning to get beyond Jim's death, something happens to make me sad all over again.*
Pastor: *What kinds of things?*
Care Receiver: *Oh, I'll come across some letters he wrote to me while he was in the army, or a friend will remind me of the wonderful time we all had together at the lake, or one of the kids will write from college about how much he's missing Dad. And then I'll just start crying all over again as if I can't stop.*
Pastor: *At those times, what seems to help the most?*
Care Receiver: *I guess just knowing that I'll be able to talk about it. I get so much from your visits. But ...*
Pastor: *But . . . .?*

Care Receiver: *But I know that you have to spend time with others who've just lost loved ones. We've had three funeral services at the church in just the past few days. And you've been wonderful in the ways you've been with those families.*

Pastor: *I appreciate your saying that. Yes, we do have a lot of needs in the parish that I have to attend to, and you're right that I will be spending more time with others in the next few weeks. But that doesn't have to mean that you won't have someone to talk with the way that you've been talking to me.*

Care Receiver: *(tearfully) It doesn't?*

Pastor: *No. We're blessed in our church to have a number of well-trained lay shepherds who minister to people in all sorts of situations. I have someone in mind right now whom I believe would be very helpful to you and who can be available to you for however long the two of you agree on. Would you be willing to receive her as your lay shepherd?*

Care Receiver: *Yes, I would! I know I need someone right now.*

Pastor: *I'll call her as soon as I get back to the office, tell her just a little about you, and ask her to call you before the day is out. Then you and she can work out when to get together.*

Care Receiver: *I'll be looking forward to hearing from her. But does this mean that you and I can't talk anymore at all?*

Pastor: *Absolutely not. You will have someone else as your primary caregiver as you continue to deal with your husband's death, but I'm still your pastor, and I will be here for you, too.*

Care Receiver: *That's really very reassuring, and I'm grateful to you. But I'm also eager to meet my new caregiver!*

Pastor: *Great!*

The lay shepherd this pastor has in mind has been trained to help people in the kinds of circumstances with which this care receiver is dealing. And this is as it should be. A lay shepherd is carefully selected for the task by a coordinator, clergy or lay, who has tried to determine the best personal fit possible, given all the lay shepherds who may be available for assignment. As in the case just described, the potential care receiver will express to the coordinator a willingness to accept the ministry of a lay shepherd. When that happens, the assigned shepherd initiates the contact, usually by telephone, and in the ensuing face-to-face conversation seeks to build the kind of trust that will lead to an effective caring relationship. Sometimes, however, things do not go as smoothly as the dialogue quoted might lead us to expect.

IT ISN'T ALWAYS EASY

Shepherd (Trudy): *Mrs. Jones? My name is Trudy Ellison from the church. I believe Pastor Butler has mentioned me to you. This morning he called to tell me that you are willing to visit with one of our church's lay shepherds, and that he thinks I might be the person who could be of help to you right now.*

Mrs. Jones: *Well, last night he did bring up that his time was pretty scarce and that he wanted me to talk with someone else about what's going on with me these days.*

Trudy: *How did you feel when he said that to you?*

Mrs. Jones: *Like my problems weren't important to him! Oh dear, I shouldn't be talking like that. Our pastor is a very busy man. He works so hard, and I know that there must be a lot of people who need him more than I should.*

Trudy: *It hurt you that you wouldn't be able to talk to him. You felt you needed him and not someone else.*

Mrs. Jones: *Yes. Do you think I'm being selfish to feel that way?*

Trudy: *It sounds to me like you were feeling disappointed. I don't see that as being selfish.*

Mrs. Jones: *Well, I do need to talk with somebody about my husband's death, and from what you've said so far, I think I'd like to talk with you.*

Trudy: *I have time this afternoon. Would it be convenient if I came to your home?*

Mrs. Jones: *I have a doctor's appointment this afternoon, but anytime tomorrow would be wonderful. I don't know whether we could get enough peace and quiet here, though. I still have family members staying with me, and it seems as if there are children everywhere!*

Trudy: *How about our getting together tomorrow morning at ten, at my house? It's very quiet around here that time of day.*

Mrs. Jones: *I'd like to come then. Would you tell me how to get to your house?*

Trudy: *(gives directions) I'm really looking forward to meeting you.*

Mrs. Jones: *I'll see you tomorrow!*

As experienced lay shepherds will recognize immediately, this is a rather typical interchange. Whenever a pastor or trusted church staff member raises the possibility that ministry to a hurting parishioner continue under the auspices of a lay caregiver, and there is even a hint given that the parishioner may be getting handed off, the lay shepherd can expect some rough going when he or she tries to establish initial contact. In the first case, the pastor handled the referral well, leaving his parishioner reassured of his continuing presence in her life, even as he dealt honestly with her about the constraints on his time. The lay shepherd he asked to help will in all likelihood find it relatively easy to establish good contact early on.

In this second case, things do not go quite as smoothly. There is at least some evidence that the parishioner experienced her pastor's attempt at referring her to a lay shepherd as somewhat abrupt. But Trudy compensated well, respecting what Mrs. Jones was experiencing, encouraging her to express her feelings without taking personal offense, and thereby opening the door to developing mutual trust. As soon as Mrs. Jones was ready to consider a face-to-face meeting, Trudy immediately scheduled it at a time convenient to both. Though the pastor in this case may have come across as less patient with Mrs. Jones than he might have—we do not know for sure—what he did do that facilitated a good contact between the parishioner and the lay shepherd was to move quickly. Less than a day passed between his talking to Mrs. Jones and his asking the lay shepherd to follow up. The lay shepherd acted quickly, also. What could have been a collapse of care ministry turned into a productive and helpful relationship out of which a lasting friendship developed. Unfortunately for another potential care receiver, things did not go so well.

Shepherd (Steve): *Hello, Mr. Brown. I'm Steve Smith, a lay shepherd at the church. Our minister of education called me last week to ask if I could be available to you. I understand one of your teenage sons has gotten back on drugs.*

Mr. Brown: *Well, I sure could use some help. Reverend Allen told me you've had some experience working with families like ours. We were hoping to hear from you before this.*

Steve: *Oh, I'm really sorry about that. We've had family for the holidays and it's really been a zoo around here. It'll be so good to get some peace and quiet again.*

Mr. Brown: *I don't want to be another burden on you. Maybe we ought to look around for some professional counseling.*

Steve: *You wouldn't be a burden. But I can understand your wanting to think about going a different route. Look, if you ever think I can be of help, though, all you have to do is give me a call. Okay?*

Mr. Brown: *Thanks.*

Steve: *Don't mention it.*

Later on Mr. Brown did mention it to the minister of education. The leadership team of the congregation's lay shepherding ministry then promptly scheduled a review session with all the lay shepherds on the process of making effective contact with potential care receivers.

As we draw this chapter to a close, we need to underscore how vital to effective shepherding establishing contact is. Though the other eight techniques, interventions, or kinds of response that we will look at have their own roles to play in our caring for people, none has quite the kind of place that this first one does. If we do not expeditiously establish contact with another in need, we likely will be unable to do anything else on his or her behalf. As we have seen, the shepherding relationship poses a somewhat different cluster of potential obstacles to establishing contact than does most any other kind of caring relationship. But whatever the obstacle in whatever kind of caring, it will have to be overcome for effective caring even to begin.

SOME QUESTIONS TO THINK ABOUT

1. How easy or difficult is it for you to form new friendships? What makes the process go best for you?
2. You have just gotten off the phone with your pastor, who has asked you to be a shepherd to Mr. Cooper, an elderly member of the congregation. Mr. Cooper's wife died two weeks ago. Think about and write out what you would say to Mr. Cooper when you call him to set up your first caregiving session.
3. Suppose that Mr. Cooper's response to your call is something like this: *Oh, I know that the pastor thinks I need to talk with someone, but I'm getting along all right by myself. I thank you for taking time to call me, though.* What kinds of feelings can you imagine yourself having? Think about and write out what would you now say to Mr. Cooper.
4. Suppose that Mr. Cooper is so eager to talk about what has happened that his words start tumbling out. You feel that it would be better to be listening to him face to face. How would you go about communicating your wanting to hear more and at the same time your desire to meet him personally before getting into too much? Write out what you might say to him.

10. Listen before You Leap, and Then Listen Some More

O F ALL THE SKILLS WE MUST LEARN IN ORDER TO BE SOMEONE'S SHEPHERD, none will prove more helpful and appreciated than listening. Listening, however, sometimes turns out to be the hardest part of our work. Why? Because we are too often preoccupied with what interests, stresses, excites, and delights us to take much note of what interests, stresses, excites, and delights others, even those we especially care about and love. When we are self-absorbed, we do not listen well—or at all. In spite of ourselves, however, we can learn to listen more and to listen better, and as a result become more effective in expressing care to others. Preparing ourselves to listen well is the subject of this chapter.

FOCUSING ON THE OTHER
What does it take to be a good listener? It takes a commitment to put other people's concerns ahead of our own, a willingness to set aside what we would like to talk about in order to concentrate on what others might like to talk about with us. In order to listen well in any particular situation, we must develop a genuine interest in what people want and need to share wherever we encounter them—whether at home, work, church, school, the gas station, doctors' offices, airports, the check-out line at the grocery store, and every other place. When we listen from interest rather than from obligation, we are better able to respond thoughtfully and appropriately, in ways that encourage them to share even more.

Little of what has just been said about listening suggests that becoming a good listener is a matter of mastering certain techniques. Instead, we are talking about a basic attitude or mindset in relating to people. When we truly listen to someone, we open ourselves to cherish everything that he or she is feeling, thinking about, anguishing over, anticipating, fearfully avoiding, and celebrating. And though we hold up our end of the conversation, we also weigh carefully what we say. We think before we speak. For we meet not to do much talking ourselves but rather to hear and care about what the other has to say, no matter where the conversation may lead. Listening in these senses is what shepherding is mostly about.

"You're kidding!" one layperson said to me, when I had made this point. "That's all? Why, I can do that. A piece of cake!" He soon found out that listening was the hardest thing he had ever done to try to help someone. Most times he was preoccupied with doing something for the other, especially something Christian. Time and time again, his peers reminded him, he was failing to do the one thing most needed: to offer himself as someone ready and willing to listen, just to listen, really to listen—and listen, and listen.

It isn't easy to do this, at least for most of us. When we genuinely listen to another, we must enter the other's world on the other's terms, to understand how things seem from his or her perspective rather than from our own. However uncomfortable we may get in the process, we must strive to overcome every urge to evade or avoid the other's self-disclosures. We do not take over the conversation, or hurry it along, or try to steer it in directions more to our liking. And since one or the other of these urges usually makes its presence felt at one moment or another in most shepherding conversations, our efforts to resist them will have to be constant. The energy required for successful resistance will be considerable. But the rewards will be great. Most times we will find ourselves appreciating more and more our new and cherished companion in Christ. And we will enjoy more and more a mutuality bounded by solicitude, prayer, gratitude, love, and service.

HOW NOT TO LISTEN WELL

Though it is mutually uplifting when people genuinely listen to one another, such listening is rare, precisely because it runs against our self-centeredness. We need not be overly puzzled and disconcerted that most relationships, even caring relationships, seem so conspicuously lacking in the listening dimension. Or that what all too often passes for listening are conventional, stereotypical, banal reactions that the indifferent, distracted, and self-absorbed toss half-heartedly and only vaguely in each other's direction.

Sam: *Since I lost my job, I've been at my wit's end trying to figure out how I'm going to take care of my family.*

Ed: *Oh, things like this are always scary at first, but you will do all right.*

Sam: *Yeah, I've gotta get out there and pound some pavement. There are plenty of opportunities just waiting for me.*

Ed: *So don't let things get you down—everything will be better soon.*

Sam: *God helps those who help themselves, right?*

Ed: *Right on!*

Or still further, some conversations become overwhelmed by hurried, deprecating, intimidating comments that the impatient, controlling, and hostile impose on those whom they experience only as bothers.

Tess: *Everyone's against me. Nothing I do is right, no matter how hard I try, and nobody will help me do my job better. I'm sick and tired of this whole thing.*

Ginny: *Here we go again! If you don't stop this whining and moaning, the whole office is going to revolt against you. Quit complaining, put a smile on your face, and just get on with it!*

Even Christian shepherds from time to time become tempted to react to their care receivers with something that falls short of attentive listening. Their patience, too, can run out. They, too, can reach the point of not wanting to hear any more:

I like my care receiver a lot, but I swear, if he starts in one more time about how his father always used to call him a lazy bum, I'm going to cuss at him, or head for my car.

Well-trained and adequately nurtured lay shepherds, however, no matter how on the edge they may feel, temper their impulses to throw listening to the winds. They can stop themselves from venting their feelings on their care receivers. Nevertheless, the fact that they must constantly work at it is strong evidence for saying that it is difficult to become consistently and enthusiastically a genuinely caring listener.

Given a commitment to become a better listener, what can help are training, practice, and supervision in a supportive but also challenging and sometimes even confrontative atmosphere. Many programs offer such training, and it is a matter for celebration that so many churches not only are aware of them but also utilize them on a continuing basis. We can learn to listen more and better, and our learning can have lasting consequences for our personal relationships and for our ministry to others. The image of

God in each of us, which constitutes our humanness, includes a rich and encompassing set of capacities to represent our Creator in the created order. It includes especially the capacity to communicate, share, and achieve lasting community and communion with others. Thus, for all of the self-centeredness we have, we also have come into the world with an aptitude for listening caringly to another. Properly nurtured and personally cultivated, that aptitude can become a well-developed skill.

JUST LISTEN!

For most people, even the first hint that another stands ready to listen is enough to open, if not a torrent, at least a stream of self-disclosure that tends to widen and deepen with every positive gesture of response. Anything and everything may tumble out before an attentive listener—joys, sorrows, worries, complaints, fantasies, requests, hopes, confessions, plans—almost always in proportion to the genuineness of the listening response. Most of our conversations with those we shepherd, therefore, are not made up of the time-passing chitchat that characterizes so many of our other relationships. When they become so, it is usually because we have not yet made the kind of contact and connection we looked at in the previous chapter. Shepherding is serious business. We listen, together, for the movement of the Spirit. And this is what finally makes it easier. As hard as it is to listen, when we do listen, the importance of what we are doing becomes so clear as to be positively motivating and personally enriching.

There is, however, another side to this. The ultimate aim of listening is for us to hear what is beyond, behind, and beneath surface disclosures, what another is trying to get at more than what his or her words convey literally, explicitly, and directly. But unless there is also a serious listening to the surface disclosures and a respectful response to them, whatever skills we may have to help another explore deeper terrain may never come into play. The most frequent cause of failure to listen is an unwillingness just to listen. The key to good shepherding is not to discourage all casual conversation but rather to discern the right moment for encouraging care receivers to tell us a little more about what is really going on with them. Let's take a little closer look at this kind of encouragement.

If the most frequent cause of shepherding mishaps is the failure to establish a relationship of trust, then the most frequent cause of the latter is the failure just to listen and really to listen to the other. In a word: listen a lot, and talk only a little. To be sure, a well-prepared shepherd has much to say to another who is seeking his or her help. What is said, however, will mean more to the other when less of it is said than the shepherd may want to say, feels obligated to say, or perhaps even is inspired to say.

Silence, however, is not always a sign of another's listening. It can be a disguise for inattention, indifference, boredom, or contempt. Similarly, speaking is not always a sign that the speaker is not listening; often, saying something is the only way to indicate that one is listening. Though there are many ways to indicate attentiveness to another without saying any-thing—namely, gestures, body language, and facial expressions—words are especially powerful vehicles for expressing a listener's genuine desire to hear more and to understand better what has already been shared. By carefully chosen words, we can affirm the other as someone who matters, who is important, who is worthy of being heard, who has something to say worth saying, and who has a life to live that is worth living to the fullest.

Sometimes our words take the form of invitations just to say more so that the shepherd can keep on listening:

> *Okay ...*
> *Hmm ...*
> *Tell me more.*
> *Can you fill that out a little for me?*
> *Could you explain in a little more detail?*

Or we may restate what we think the other has been saying to us, to make sure that we are hearing what he or she wants to say and to offer another opportunity for the other to elaborate the story further:

> *I've heard you saying ... have I got it right?*
> *If I understand you correctly, the issue for you is ...*

Sometimes, as a part of our listening, we may attempt to summarize what has been said to us, to show that what we have heard matters enough to try to get to the heart of it and that we know there may be more to be said about the matter:

> *You were mad when she ...*
> *What really matters to you in all this is that ...*
> *You're frustrated working so hard to ... and not measuring up to your own standards for success.*
> *Right now it seems to you that your life would get better if he would change, and you get sad when you realize that he's not going to do it.*

Both lay and professional caregivers must be able to communicate effec-tively that they are listening and listening well if they are to have any hope of doing anything else worthwhile for a care receiver. As the previous examples illustrate, some of the best ways of doing this include

- encouraging the other to keep talking;
- checking out whether we are following correctly what he or she is saying and trying to say;
- asking for further information; and
- summarizing what has been said.

Curiously, though, listening without saying much is often enough to do.

There is something profoundly paradoxical about good listening. When we listen to others for the sake of the listening, we may do more for them than we could possibly do otherwise, without doing anything other than listening. Listening conveys commitment, steadfastness, and trustworthiness. It expresses not only the caring spirit of the listener but also the transforming power of the communities the listener represents, whether a family, a neighborhood, the guild of competent mental health professionals, or a Spirit-filled community of faith filled with love and gratitude for what God is doing in the world. Listening says to the other that I am here with you and that I will be here with you, no matter what.

Listening promises no rescues, answers, solutions, or cures. It promises only presence—respectful, caring, attentive, patient, prayerful, hopeful presence. But in rendering this, listening makes present, in the midst of another's fears and hopes, the being of God as the One whose name is not only I AM but I WILL BE THERE. The heart of all shepherding in our Father's name is our promise to remain open, respectful, and caring, no matter what another may choose to share with us next: *Say more. I'm here to listen. And I'm here for you.*

Listening and being listened to are powerful symbols of the nature of the relationship between every human being and God the Creator. By inviting us to give prayerful utterance to our deepest wants and needs (*Luke 11:9-10*), God, like our shepherds, listens to us before acting on our behalf. Sometimes, God's letting us know that he is listening can be more important than anything else God may do for us.

A TIME TO SPEAK

We must consider briefly a shepherding situation in which listening, for all its importance most everywhere else, may not be the best course of caring action. The situation is provoked by significant loss. Confronted by loss— of a home, a career, a relationship, or of a loved one—people typically react with some combination of shock, anxiety, confusion, grief, sadness, and depression. At such times they tend to find that talking with people, even with those who are the most concerned about them, is too hard. And it should not be asked of them. As a preacher long ago said, there is a time for silence as well as a time for speaking (*Ecclesiastes 3:7*).

It will help our care receivers, however, to get their feelings out. In times of loss they deserve a shepherd's gentle encouragement to do so, for the sake of their healing. But "gentle" must be the shepherd's watchword. An understanding shepherd will know that for a time he or she may have to do more talking than would be helpful in many other situations—but never just to fill the silence. Silences still must be honored. When people are truly depressed, though, they need fewer of them. The ruminations that they get into in the midst of silences can impede their moving beyond a loss toward renewed involvement in other relationships. When we shepherd people in situations of loss, we must become more active—and even talkative—than we are in most of our caregiving. In doing so, though, we must never lose sight of the general principle that good listening is vital to good shepherding.

SOME QUESTIONS TO THINK ABOUT

1. What in your life do you most enjoy talking about with others?
2. What do you typically do when you begin to get the impression that others are not as interested as you are in what you have been saying to them?
3. What helps you the most to listen well to someone else? What makes such listening the most difficult for you?

11. Sacred Secrecy: Confidentiality and the Shepherding Relationship

DURING THE FIRST CENTURIES OF THE CHURCH'S HISTORY, A PROBLEM AROSE for shepherds of souls that proved especially vexing. It had to do with postbaptismal sins. Of particular concern was the sin of failing to be faithful to the gospel in times of persecution. The problem resulted from the way the church had come to understand baptism as a remission of sin.

For our purposes, the relevant ingredients of that understanding are that those who receive baptism are freed from the consequences of every sin of omission and commission in our lives prior to baptism and that there is only one baptism for the remission of those consequences. On these terms, as forgiven sinners, our new relation to God will remain intact forever, so long as we commit no further sin. If we should sin in some way, however, there would be no remedy, since we cannot be baptized again.

It is little wonder that some people began seriously to contemplate putting off baptism until the last moment of their lives! Peculiar as their thinking might seem, it was realistic about the fruits of baptism. For whatever else our baptism may do for us, it will not prevent us from sinning further.

Is there any other way of dealing with the inevitability of postbaptismal sinning than by cannily crafting the right time to die and then hastily receiving the rite of baptism? As church leaders wrestled with this issue, they began to appreciate again the gospel message of the forgiveness of sin as God's promised response whenever repentance and confession are in evidence. Especially interesting is the view of confession that emerged. The confession of postbaptismal sin that was to be part of the sinner's eventual restoration to Christian fellowship was public confession. Only a public confession, it came to be believed, could allow the community of believers to forgive the sinner whom God already had forgiven.

In subsequent centuries, repentance and confession remained the principal means by which Christians dealt with the sins they committed after being baptized. But confession gradually became a matter between the individual penitent and a priest who was under a holy obligation never to reveal the contents of any confession. In the fullest sense of the term, confession became private rather than public. Secrets revealed to a priest in the confessional were to be regarded as sealed from others' knowledge forever.

The tradition of the seal of the confessional laid the foundation for the principle of confidentiality that governs virtually all modern caregiving. In the next paragraphs, I will attempt to summarize what this principle has come to mean for the ministry of shepherding, first at the level of principle only. Then I will introduce the exceptions to its application that are currently required for responsible caregiving.

IT'S BETWEEN YOU AND ME

Whatever we may think about the process by which public confession became a private transaction involving two people, from that process has arisen a responsibility that none of us is at liberty to overlook in our shepherding. We are to keep everything shared by our care receivers in confidence, as for our ears only. Note especially the reference to everything.

Not only is a care receiver's explicit sharing and confessing of a sin to be held confidential; whatever else he or she may say during the course of our conversations must remain between us also. We do not have the right to share with anyone else, except our referral source, even the bare fact that we are any particular person's shepherd. Our care receivers may and often do reveal that we are their shepherds. And they have the right to do so. But we do not.

Of course, we not only may but also should share something of our ministering on a regular basis with our peer shepherds and our leaders, in order better to ensure the highest quality of caring on everyone's part. At the same time, however, we are under obligation to take every action possible to prevent our colleagues from recognizing who our care receiver is even as we receive needed consultation about and supervision of our work. This is why every responsible program of lay shepherding training will include information about how to de-identify care receivers during the supervision process. One way is to refer to our care receiver as "care receiver" or "CR." Another is to give a fictitious name that we identify as such to those reviewing our ministering. This has been the procedure followed in this book; the vignettes presented are typical in the experience of lay shepherds, but the names are not those of the participants. For me it is easier to talk about issues when I can refer to my care receiver by some name:

Tonight I want to share some of my ministering to a man I'll call Jack.

As we would know, Jack isn't his real name ...

In many instances, the identity of a care receiver might become known immediately to the members of a peer support or supervision group unless we make other changes in the presentation of data. Our commitment to confidentiality mandates that we make such changes also:

... and for the purposes of our discussion, I am going to say that he has been in the hospital because of a heart condition and that what's bothering him especially is an unresolved conflict with his older son ...

The care receiver in this case was a man struggling with diabetes and taking care of his elderly father with whom he had had conflicts since childhood.

It is not easy to juggle our need to present an accurate picture of our shepherding so that we can get the help we need and our obligation to protect those we talk about from being recognized by anyone else. However, we have no choice but to struggle with the dilemma. Practice does make our task easier, as does securing a commitment from all members of our peer group to maintain confidentiality when on a rare occasion they may realize whom we are talking about.

All of our care receivers have the right to receive our assurance and pledge that we will not reveal anything that they say to us, and we have the obligation to provide that assurance and pledge at the earliest possible moment of our ministering to them. Violating this principle will destroy the trust that is necessary to any caring relationship. If we violate this principle, we will destroy the relationship. In many cases, violating the principle of confidentiality will also harm the care receiver in ways that may permit him or her to hold our churches and us accountable, perhaps even in a court of law. In short, maintaining confidences is serious business. Everyone loses when a confidence is breached.

WHEN A CONFIDENCE MUST BE REVEALED

Can there be any exception(s) to the principle of confidentiality? The professional ethics statements of most associations of mental health professionals, along with state laws, generally affirm two kinds of exceptions. We have the right and the obligation to break confidences that contain clear indications that our care receiver may commit suicide or may be ready to do significant harm to himself or herself, or that he or she is about to do significant harm to someone else. Fortunately—or, better, providentially—only rarely does a lay shepherd have to confront such horrific possibilities. But if such should ever arise, he or she must contact the referral coordinator or supervisor immediately, so that plans for appropriate additional interventions can be worked out and implemented quickly. In conversation with the person threatening the harmful act, the lay shepherd should indicate his or her duty to act in the best interest of the care receiver at all times, even if it should require breaking a confidence. Also, the shepherd should indicate what kinds of action he or she will take if there is any doubt about the care receiver's readiness to inflict harm.

We can be grateful that in many situations that may seem ominous at the outset, the danger can be averted with sensitive caregiving. Consider, for example, the following vignette:

Joe: *I can't seem to make anything go right anymore. Nobody around here has a clue about how bad things have gotten in my life … how tired I am … how lonely I am.… Who would ever want to be around me now anyway? I don't see any way out of the mess I've made of everything. Sometimes I wonder if I wouldn't be better off dead.*

Shepherd: *Joe, you have at least one person who wants to be here for you right now—me. But what you've said about being better off dead worries me. Could you clue me in a little more about that?*

Joe: *I couldn't feel any worse than I do now, and if I left my car running in the garage some night I at least wouldn't be feeling this way anymore.*

Shepherd: *Joe, you may have something when you say that you aren't going to feel any worse. But I believe you've got it in you, with God's help, to make things better before you leave this world on his terms rather than yours.*

Joe: *Right now, I wouldn't even know where to start.*

Shepherd: *Right now, I don't either. But an hour from now, we might. Want to have a go at it?*

Joe: *You really think you can stand it?*

Shepherd: *You better believe it.*

It may turn out that Joe's shepherd will deem it necessary to call for more help. But for now it seems that Joe is showing the beginnings of a willingness to work on his problems rather than escaping them through a self-destructive act. Imagine this same conversation taking a somewhat different turn:

Shepherd: ... *But I believe you've got it in you, with God's help, to make thing better ...*

Joe: *God went out of my life a long time ago. And I just haven't got anything left in me that can help. What's kept me from snuffing myself out has been the fear of dying alone. And I've gotten over that. I want out.*

Now the shepherd is in a different situation. Further conversation alone may not reduce Joe's pain enough to prevent him from going ahead with his clear and easily implementable plan to take his own life. However abrupt it may be to the flow of things to this point in the caregiving, his shepherd must immediately initiate a shift in course. Here is one way to go about it:

Shepherd: *Joe, I don't want to believe it, but I have to—you look to me like a man who is about to do something terrible to himself. And it scares me and it makes me sad, because I know that I don't have the power to stop you if you decide to go through with this. But I love you, Joe, and I've got to do everything I can to get some help for you for those times that you might not be able to stop yourself. Who can we get over here to stay with you when I'm not here?*

Joe: *Nobody who would care.*

Shepherd: *They wouldn't come if they didn't care, Joe.*

Joe: *Well, my brother and his wife live about an hour from here. We never got along too well, though.*

Shepherd: *Would he come? Would they come?*

Joe: *Yeah, they'd come.*

Shepherd: *Let's call them.*

While Joe and his shepherd wait for the brother's arrival, their conversation includes the following:

Shepherd: *I'm really glad your brother is on his way, Joe. After he gets here and we visit together a little while, I'll take my leave. But I'll be back tomorrow. And I'll call you tonight. If you feel that you'd like me to talk with you before then, I want you to promise now that you'll call me right away. We can talk on the phone, or I'll come over. Meantime, I'm going to touch base with Reverend Taylor, who first suggested to us both that we might work together. I want to make sure that I'm doing everything that I can for you right now, because I know we're into some real rough times.*

Joe: *When you talk with him, tell him thanks. I need you both. And I appreciate you both.*

Shepherd: *He'll be glad to hear that from you, just as I am.*

Much of what is in evidence in this case of a suicidal care receiver bears considerable similarity with how dialogue with a violent person goes. The shepherd must find a way quickly to inform the care receiver of the duty to warn the person who is at risk, to begin involving others in helping to prevent the particular threat from being carried out, and to communicate an abiding concern to help the care receiver bring his or her presently dangerous level of anger under reliable control. Obviously, in the case of a violent care receiver, the shepherd must also do whatever is needed by way of self-protection. Precisely because these two situations occur so rarely in lay caregiving, it may be easy for shepherds to forget what they should have been trained to do when one or the other does arise. Periodic review, perhaps accompanied by some role playing, can be an important topic for their ongoing continuing education program.

In bringing this chapter to a close, we return to its main orientation: In almost all lay shepherding, as in almost all professional care rendering, the obligation to maintain strict confidentiality is beyond debate. Most shepherds will never find themselves in situations that are exceptions to this vitally important principle or rule. It is, however, important to remember that these exceptions exist, and it is important to know how to deal with them on the extremely rare occasions when they occur.

SOME QUESTIONS TO THINK ABOUT

1. Have you ever told someone something in confidence, only to discover later that the confidence was not kept? How did you feel after the discovery? What were some of the repercussions of the violation?
2. Consider the following situations, which are fairly typical for lay shepherds. How would you respond in each scenario?

- After the church service one Sunday, a fellow worshiper comes to you and asks: *Say, you've been talking with Fred lately as his lay shepherd, haven't you?*
- A good friend sees you in the grocery store, comes over to you, and says: *It's just wonderful that you've been talking with Mary. She's feeling so good about your work with her.*
- The son of your elderly and seriously ill care receiver approaches you following your session with his father and asks you: *Do you think Dad is any less angry with us for raising the possibility of putting him in a nursing home?*
- Your spouse calls you to the phone: *It's Susie, for you again. Isn't she the one you've been shepherding at the church?*

12. Responding to Feelings: the Transforming Power of Mirroring

Let your words always be gracious, ...
learn how best to respond to each person you meet.
(Colossians 4:6, REB)

F OR MORE THAN HALF A CENTURY, NO ADEQUATE COURSE OF TRAINING
for pastoral care and counseling has omitted the methods of the client-centered therapy developed by Carl Rogers. Though few therapists and counselors call themselves Rogerian anymore, most integrate Rogers's insights with everything else they provide their clients. Those insights have filtered downward from professional training programs to assume a central role in the equipping of lay caregivers.

At the heart of Rogers's approach to helping people is an unshakeable confidence in the power of a warm, respectful, empathic counselor to stimulate growth and healing in others by listening carefully and acceptingly and by reflecting what he or she hears without analysis, interpretation, concurrence, judgment, advice, or commentary. Rogerian treatment is not a matter of applying sophisticated techniques that only expertly trained and exquisitely skilled therapists have at their disposal. Rather, it is a matter of therapists' offering empathy—and the humanness underlying it—for the sake of helping distressed persons see and appreciate better the healing resources residing within themselves. From the standpoint of the theological tradition that seemed to give Rogers so much difficulty, what best helps us to heal is the experience of another who has our own genuine well-being at heart: the greatest of all gifts is love.

IS EMPATHY ENOUGH?

The hallmark of Rogers-influenced caregiving is patient accepting and reflecting of peoples' feelings without attempting to do anything more, trusting throughout that this will be enough. As everyone who has received any training in such an approach soon learns, this is not easy. Most times we bring to our shepherding the distractions of our own lives, our hard-won convictions about what others need, and our shaky egos demanding success in whatever we undertake. It is difficult to filter out all this background noise for the sake of deep listening. Given all the distractions that we bring to our caring for others, it is not easy to trust that the process of reflecting represents all that most people need. We think we must do more.

Another reason why many caregivers may have difficulty applying Rogers's principles to caring for others is that they do not hold the uncompromisingly positive outlook on human nature that rooted so deeply in Rogers's soul. Because they do not, they cannot believe as Rogers did that sources of healing are available within each person and that those sources are never so corrupted as to be inaccessible to another's warmth, empathy, and unconditional positive regard. It is sad that Rogers found it necessary to separate himself from the Christian tradition on this issue. Apparently he identified the whole of Christianity with its somber post-Augustinian formulations of original sin and total depravity. Finding it necessary (and rightly so) to reject these specific formulations, Rogers wrongly rejected the Christian tradition as a whole, with its strong emphasis on the indestructibility of the divine image in humanity, even after the Fall, and on the perfectibility of human beings through divine grace. However, many people in our churches continue to look at human nature in the way so inimical to Rogers's best insights.

A third difficulty in employing Rogerian methods is that it is hard to pay attention to people no matter what, to listen to them instead of waiting to tell them something, and to accept them in whatever condition they may be in—physically, emotionally, mentally, or spiritually. Also, it is hard to put ourselves out for others whether or not we like them and whether or not we like making ourselves available to them. For many would-be shepherds, this requirement is too much to handle. A dogged commitment to do the right thing for others and some training in how best to offer them care may be of some help. But for people who at best only tolerate others, nothing short of conversion—literally, a remaking of their fundamental attitudes and perspective—is likely to bring about the change of heart necessary to be an effective shepherd.

The central technique of Rogerian client-centered or nondirective therapy is often referred to as the accepting acknowledgment and nonjudgmental reflecting of a client's feelings. Its fundamental presupposition is that in a warm, respectful and, in the language of faith, grace-filled environment people can come to understand and appreciate the insights and the energy for positive change that reside within themselves. The most important term in this characterization is reflection, and with it an implied analogy to mirroring. In the following paragraphs, I want to draw from this analogy more than its suggestions for responding to others' feelings. As shepherds we are called to respond to another's whole selfhood and to find ways of expressing God's love for him or her not only as a person with feelings but also as a person. Communicating an acceptance of people's feelings is an important part of the communication process, but it is not the whole of it.

I SEE YOU SEEING ME

As everyone knows who has seen outrageous images on funhouse mirrors, accurate reflecting requires an instrument fashioned with some care. Not just any sort of shiny surface will do. When an instrument is well crafted and polished for the purpose, nothing on or behind its mirrored surface distorts the representation of what stands before it. A good mirror gives back only what light conveys to it. The most important implication of these observations is that for an image in a mirror to change, that which produces the image must change first.

Some people use their mirrors only as instruments of self-admiration. But mirrors can be used for something much more important. They can show us what we might change about ourselves. If our image shines clearly enough on the mirror's surface, then what we can choose to change about that image will become apparent, sometimes painfully so. Here is a somewhat superficial illustration:

> Oh my, this haircut doesn't do anything like what I thought it was going to. I'm going to have to shorten it a lot more on the sides.

A similarly superficial response, focused only on feelings, might be this:

> You're disappointed that your hair doesn't look the way you wanted.

A mirroring response, by contrast, goes deeper, seeking the person behind the surface image:

It seems to concern you a lot how you look to others.

One other consideration about mirrors and our relationship to them is that mirrors only help us to see ourselves as others see or might see us. In this sense, it is true that the mirror doesn't lie. Only we can decide what, if anything, we want to do about what we see in the mirror. Mirrors reflect, but they do not analyze and they do not prescribe.

We can use many analogies from what we know about the reflecting surfaces of mirrors to enhance our understanding of the shepherding process. The most important analogy is this: becoming a good shepherd is like smoothing out the edges and rough surfaces of our personhood so as not to distort what others can discover about themselves in our responses to their disclosures. If we are accurate mirrors, others will discover important things about themselves in our responses to them, responses mirrored in our gestures, body language, and faces. In the following example, the words John uses suggest that his lay shepherd has made of himself a good and reliable mirror:

John: *And so, I've lied my way through school, been unfaithful to my wife, and I'm passing company secrets to our major competitor.*

Shepherd: *I know.*

John: *How can you just sit there calmly when I tell these horrible things about myself?*

Shepherd: *I guess it's because I see more in you than you're seeing in yourself right now.*

John: *And it's all bad.*

Shepherd: *I wonder.*

John: *It's been hard to look you squarely in the face and tell you what I've had to tell you, but when I do I don't see shock or condemnation, like I do when I stare at myself in the mirror each morning while shaving.*

Shepherd: *What do you see instead on my face?*

John: *I see concern ... kindness ... hope.*

Shepherd: *How does that make you feel?*

John: *It makes me want to change ... to make things better, for me, my wife and kids, my boss ...*

Shepherd: *What kind of an expression do you think might be on God's face now as he looks at you?*

John: *(choking back tears) I think it might be like yours.*

As this brief conversation shows, listening from a shepherding perspective involves far more than making ourselves into a kind of receptacle for containing the other's concerns, absorbing them only long enough to give them back unchanged by means of statements that merely repeat what the other has already said:

Shepherd: *John, you're feeling pretty bad about yourself right now.*

We have no choice but to begin our shepherding at this level. It can be too threatening to a care receiver if we push behind surface disclosures without establishing trust. And reflecting at first just the other's surface feelings can help to build that trust. But we still need to look and listen for how our care receivers express their inner being in their outward gestures and expressions, whether we respond directly to what we see and hear or not. Eventually our responses must begin to convey a perception that there is more to our care receiver than he or she now sees and that the more is always from God. Reflecting surface feelings can leave our care receivers, like Narcissus, gazing only upon their own faces and not God's.

Many who seek help are, like Narcissus, unwilling to venture far from the pool that contains their own reflection. They are interested only in looking at themselves from their self-interested vantage points. To shift the metaphor, they want a shepherd who is willing to be for them only a sounding board, someone to bounce ideas off of. There is nothing wrong with letting ourselves become, from time to time, someone's echo chamber or backboard. Sometimes our care receivers need an opportunity to vent. The important thing to avoid is becoming only or just these things in a shepherding relationship.

BEYOND FEELINGS TO SELFHOOD

Distressed people do not get better when what comes back to them from a shepherding relationship is only what they have thrown out to the shepherd. It would be the height of folly for shepherds to presume that their sheep can find nourishment across long winters from what their stomachs contain before the winters begin. It is the shepherd's responsibility to lead the sheep to other ground, sometimes higher, sometimes lower, to find more than one kind of food. By mirroring, we do not merely reflect the feelings, thoughts, attitudes, and perspective of the other only as they have come to us, on the other's terms. Instead we reflect our seeing, in and through all that the other is willing to share with us, the other person as a particular kind of person in his and her own being. He or she is a child of God who is loved by our Creator, who bears our Creator's own image, who is liberated in Christ and empowered by the Holy Spirit to become more and more godly in love and service to others. This is not a mere seeing but a seeing as. It involves a deliberate choice on our part to look upon another with the eyes of faith. And this is what holds the promise for the other's transformation—seeing the other as our Creator sees him or her, made possible by a faith that knows that God "makes his face to shine upon us." "Seeing as" is both the basis and the most authentic expression of the kinds of interventions frequently referred to in pastoral counseling literature as affirming, reassuring, and even supporting. As shepherds, we have the right and the calling to affirm to people in the name of Christ that they are beloved of God and that their future is in and with God, no matter what they may think, feel, and do or not do about life and others in it. We have the right and the calling to reassure people that God is all in all, that everything works for good to those who trust God, and that the difficulties all human beings have in sustaining such trust will never be able to separate them from the love of God manifest in Jesus Christ. And we have the right and the calling to support people by our steadfast insistence that the grace and mercy of God are available in every circumstance, however discounted, rejected, depleted, isolated, and humiliated they may feel and however hopeless their situation may seem.

We can mirror God's image of the other—and thereby render the affirmation, reassurance, and support that others have the right to expect from us—only when and because we experience God's constant and loving image of ourselves. Short of such experience, I do not know how pastors, pastoral counselors, psychotherapists, or lay shepherds can for long truly abide with—and abide at all—many of the persons for whom it is their responsibility to care. The hurts, suffering, deficits, neediness, evasiveness, demands, obstinacy, moral failures, character aberrations, and spiritual devastation in others eventually will take their toll on even the most sensitive, empathic, and patient caregivers if those caregivers try to generate from only within themselves the interest, energy, persistence, and skill necessary for effective caring. Reflecting or mirroring, without a faith-informed understanding of what the act is to convey to the other, quickly devolves into a seeing the other only as if the other is worthy of the attention, accompanied by the caregiver's anxious hoping that his or her real feelings toward the care receiver will not be found out.

As self and object relations psychologists point out, the mirroring in therapeutic interactions that proves the most helpful activates patients' memories of their most positive encounters with persons in their lives who were loving and nurturing. These persons let show on their faces and in their voices how much they meant to them, just as they are. Mirrored in the gestures, expressions, words, and caring of these significant others—parents first, one hopes—is a life-giving and sustaining judgment that the care receiver matters, is worthy of attention, respect, and care, and arouses anticipation, expectations, and hope in their caregivers, thus enhancing the quality of their own lives in manifold ways.

On the faces and in the voices of those who love us is rendered, perhaps more concretely than in any other way outside of a direct encounter with God, one of the most profound truths of faith, that we are creatures of God, already and irrevocably deemed good. It is very good that we are who we are, that we can be who we are even though we are not completely our own, and that because we have a calling to be for others as well, we need never be alone. There is nothing neutral about this kind of mirroring; it conveys from first to last a valuing of the most important kind of all, grounded in the most profound kind of reason of all: we show our love to others because God has shown love to them, and to us, first. Trusting that this is so makes the reason also a wellspring for action, sustaining an otherwise overwhelmed shepherd in respecting the disrespectful and the contemptible, remaining benevolent toward the malevolent, holding out hope for the hopeless, and loving the unloved, the unloving, and the unlovable.

SOME QUESTIONS TO THINK ABOUT

1. People express all kinds of feelings to each other: joy, sadness, peace, fear, resignation, anger, anticipation, hopelessness, to name just a few. With which of these feelings are you personally the most or the least comfortable?
2. One of the most famous blessings in the Bible is recorded in Numbers 6:24-26: "The LORD bless thee and keep thee; the LORD make his face to shine upon thee and be gracious unto thee; the LORD lift up his countenance upon thee and give thee peace" (KJV). In your life, whose faces conveyed to you most authentically the sense of grace, kindness, and peace that this blessing invokes? When in your relationships with them did you face their own blessings most keenly?
3. When in your life have you felt most strongly the affirmation, reassurance, and support of God?
4. What kinds of changes in yourself would help you most to convey a sense of God's affirmation, reassurance, and support to others?

13. Advice Giving: The Wisdom of Not Being Wise

A CARDINAL RULE OF ALL CARING IS THAT IT MUST BE DIRECTED TOWARD helping people become better at helping themselves. To be sure, distressed persons need a strong hand to hold onto as they take their first steps through a crisis or major life transition. And good shepherds intervene in their lives actively. But if the caring relationship they establish is a healthy one, the recipient eventually must grasp the importance of accepting responsibility for his or her own life, in and beyond the crisis or life transition at hand. From the perspective of faith, learning to be responsible for oneself is learning to become accountable to God. One of the most grievous errors any caregiver can make, however well-intended his or her action may be, is to give too much direction, offer too much advice, or answer too many questions that the care receiver should answer for himself or herself. Here is an extreme example of the error:

Rita: *I just don't see how we're ever going to get through this.*

Shepherd: *Well, it's obvious that you need to give that skirt-chasing husband of yours his walking papers.*

Rita: *But what about our children? They need their daddy.*

Shepherd: *Children are tough. They'll get over it.*

Or this:

George: *It seems like everything I've done lately has gone sour. There are so many things wrong in my life right now that sometimes I just feel like giving up.*

Shepherd: *George, you've got to get right with God for anything to work* *in your life. I know what I'm talking about. Let me tell you what was happening to me before I started praying and going back to church ...*

Unfortunately for George, his shepherd did tell him about his own spiritual journey—for the remainder of the time they spent together that day. Subsequently the shepherd complained uncomprehendingly to his fellow lay ministers about how hard it was trying to find a time in George's busy schedule for them to meet. As for Rita, things might have gone better for her had she adopted George's evasive strategy. Instead, in her desperation, she took her shepherd's advice, divorced her husband, and soon concluded that she had made the greatest mistake of her life.

A few well-meaning, caring people I have talked with over the years act toward others as if they have never heard that telling people what to do usually does more harm than good. Rather, they take pride in constantly being consulted by others, believing that all of their freely dispensed advice will unfailingly be of help. Even lay shepherds can occasionally feel tempted to assume the mantle of expert on things that they know are extraneous to their caregiving. Here is a sample of advice I have heard lay shepherds asked to address during the course of their ministering: whether to serve white or red wine at a dinner party; which real estate agent will sell a house faster; whether or not to try Viagra; the best arthritis medication; whether a family should add a room to their house; the cost-benefit ratio of an Ivy League education; the proper balance of stocks and bonds in an investment portfolio; medication or psychotherapy for the treatment of depression; how much life insurance to carry; fending off a potential lawsuit; buying a car for a high school graduation present; and how to avoid an IRS audit.

On some of these subjects, particular shepherds possess credentials on the basis of which they can tender an expert opinion. However, the shepherds asked to do the advising were no more qualified to offer an opinion than the person who asked for it. And on none of the subjects was the advice requested germane to the specific issues with which the helping relationship was established to deal. Offering such advice only confuses the nature of the shepherding being offered.

THE DIFFICULTIES WITH NOT GIVING ADVICE

We have ample reason to be at least as cautious as responsible therapists are when it comes to offering advice in the course of helping people. But it is not easy to sustain such caution in the context of shepherding. Consider, first, the dilemma every pastor must face. Most people who seek pastoral care and counseling bring with them high, positive expectations, both that their pastor or pastoral counselor will know what will resolve their difficulties and that what will be offered them will have nothing less than divine approval behind it. The kinds of client expectations with which most therapists deal typically do not contain anything like the enormity of the meaning, authority, and power that people can and do confer on religious experts. This does not mean that pastors and pastoral counselors are thereby mandated to do for their parishioners and clients what other therapists cannot do for theirs. The fact that someone expects something God-sent from them does not entail either that they must or can provide it. However, people do expect certain things from their pastors that typically go beyond what patients expect from their therapists. This expectation derives from the nature of the shepherding relationship. Does this have any bearing on lay shepherding? Indeed so.

From the outset, members of the Christian community have looked to spiritual people in their midst for guidance as they strive to live their faith responsibly. And they have done so out of the recognition that many of the issues with which faith-seeking people must deal are well beyond their ability to resolve on their own and all of the time. Here are a few issues that can overwhelm us without the caring presence of others who are further along in their faith journey than we might be:
• overcoming obstacles to prayer and a devotional life;
• representing the Christian faith adequately to family members, to the world beyond the family, and to followers of other religious traditions;
• caring for the severely impaired and traumatized;
• threading one's way through diverse, often confusing, and mutually exclusive approaches to the Scriptures;
• experiencing God in times of crisis, calamity, and collapse;
• fulfilling our hunger for a deeper communion with God and sense of God's presence and will in the ordinary rounds of our lives;
• reconciling the proclamation of a just, merciful, loving God with the unrelieved suffering that people encounter everywhere;
• finding the resolve to relate caringly to others when our efforts go unnoticed, unappreciated, and unreciprocated;
• discovering sources of hope in the midst of overwhelming loss; and
• healing alienated relationships in the home, workplace, church, neighborhood, and society.

Most people rightly expect to find in their churches some help with issues like these. But it is not always their pastors who are best equipped to provide the help. In matters of faith, laypeople are resourceful, too. By virtue of their openness to God's working in their lives, their persistent struggles to understand God's will more deeply, their humility before the great mysteries of human existence in the world, and their sense of God's majesty, glory, and grace in all of creation, they can listen patiently and sensitively to another's grappling with even the most profound issues of faith. They can offer more than just a thought or two for consideration and prayerful reflection. By God's grace, they are prepared and disposed to share their own faith striving—on occasion. Also by God's grace, they are without reservations about the necessity of doing so—on those occasions.

There is some common ground possible between a therapeutic and a shepherding perspective on advice. Ordinarily, for example, neither will demand that those who seek their help agree with all the suggestions they may offer them during the course of a helping relationship. (A demand for an agreement not to harm oneself or another is a notable exception to this general rule.) But both will hold those in their care responsible for weighing relevant information, for thinking carefully about the range of options that may be open at the moment, for making a decision commensurate with the values and goals articulated during the course of the conversation, and for living with the consequences of decisions made.

From the perspective of therapy, resisting the temptation to offer too much advice or any advice is usually justified in terms of the therapist's affirming and strengthening the autonomy, ego functioning, responsibility, and self-sufficiency of the other. Advice may be offered in abundance early in a course of therapy with someone immobilized by crisis, when active structuring on the part of the therapist is especially called for. Even here, however, the therapist looks forward to the patient's gradual recovery of his or her critical faculties to make use not only of any advice proffered but of all subsequent therapeutic interventions as well, on the patient's terms. By refraining from giving advice, it is argued, the therapist also retains a posture of at least relative neutrality, within limits, regarding the patient's goals and chosen means of attaining them.

WHEN WE DO ADVISE

From a shepherding perspective, offers of advice occur in a context of a shared searching out of God's will in concrete situations, of a mutual commitment to responding positively to God, of a willingness to submit every possible response to careful scrutiny and testing, and of an openness to explore the sources of resistance to living out one's faith actively. Implicit in all advice given by a shepherd is something like:

> Given that you are seeking to bring your faith actively to bear on your struggles with ... I wonder if it might be more helpful were you to ... rather than ... or ...

As in therapy, the advice given has an open-ended quality to it and is offered out of the conviction that the ultimate responsibility for accepting or rejecting it rests with the one to whom it is given. In shepherding, however, at stake is not only the other's becoming a more autonomous, self-sufficient, and responsible individual but also that person's fulfilling his or her vocation to live a life that will glorify God. From the standpoint of faith, the autonomy that is often conceived of in terms of freedom from constraints is not an end in itself but rather serves the larger purpose of human beings becoming free for greater self-giving in the name of Christ.

Though giving advice is an unavoidable part of a good shepherd's responsibilities, careful attention to the content of any proposed advice and especially to the purpose envisioned for offering it either at a particular time or at all is crucial. A great deal of the advice that caregivers may be tempted to offer, whether as a spontaneous reaction or as the result of a lifetime of experience and wisdom, has little if anything to do with the primary tasks of shepherding souls. Nevertheless, shepherds who should and usually do know better continue to offer poorly thought out, tangential, opinionated, distracting, or erroneous advice to unknowing and overly compliant persons in distress.

SETTING ASIDE OUR EXPERTISE

A final issue has to do with the temptations many laypersons may have to offer others advice within the sphere of their professional competence during the course of a shepherding relationship. One shepherd I know spent a great deal of time showing her newly widowed care receiver how to do her taxes. Another taught his care receiver how to rewire his summer cottage and never got down to dealing with the spiritual questions for which the care receiver asked help. Still another was warmly and enthusiastically praised by her care receiver not for helping her through the difficult times following a divorce but for designing a new landscaping plan for her front yard.

Many congregations are blessed with lay shepherds who are competent in a number of different fields. They may be accountants, lawyers, teachers, engineers, consultants, mechanics, career counselors, investment bankers, technicians, nurses, architects, physicians, social workers, or psychologists, to name just a few. Sometimes, someone seeking help will ask for a particular lay minister because of his or her professional expertise. And those carrying the responsibility of matching up a potential care receiver with the right shepherd may think it important to offer a particular care receiver a shepherd who can give professional advice quickly and at no cost.

One problem such a referral poses for the shepherd is increased liability: the standards of service germane to their professions will be the standards to which lay shepherds will be held accountable whenever they choose to render professional service in the context of a shepherding relationship. An even more serious problem is the threat to the integrity of the shepherding relationship. It can be difficult for a shepherd whom another appreciates for his or her professional insight to establish himself or herself as ministering to the faith needs of that other.

To lay shepherds who may be tempted to offer help in a professional capacity, my advice on the subject is simple: don't. A shepherd's professional competence and reputation is better used to help a care receiver assess who else can advise about the problems that are not at the heart of the shepherding:

Horace: *Bill, I know that your job is to help me through Gwen's death and not to be my doctor, but I was wondering if you could look over the medications I've been taking recently and tell me if there's anything about them that concerns you. For some reason, they just don't seem to be working.*

Bill: *Horace, I really appreciate your honoring my role as one of helping you with the grief you're feeling. Keeping track of your medications is important, too, and I'm glad you're giving it attention. Tell you what. Let me give you a couple of names of colleagues I trust who can help with this while we keep working on what we've started.*

It is not always this easy. But sensitive, caring, and competent professional persons bear the responsibility of interpreting, as needed, the difference between being a consultant and being a shepherd to their care receivers. When they offer clarifications gently and respectfully but firmly, the relationship generally gets back on track relatively quickly. And shepherding can continue. The following conversation illustrates the process.

Anne: *Jean, I don't see how I'll ever get over the hurt my oldest daughter caused me by taking her children away from me.*

Jean: *From what you've you told me, I wonder if she had much of a choice about moving. When Bill left her, you said, the only job she could find required transferring to—.*

Anne: *I told her a thousand times she could move the family into this house. Goodness knows it's big enough for all of us. Her father left us well* off; Jane doesn't have to work. She's doing all this to spite me. She has always been uppity to me, no matter what I've tried to do for her. She was a daddy's girl and never had much appreciation for me. She knows how lonely I am now and how much I need my grandchildren near me.

Jean: She owes you?

Anne: Yes! But she's incapable of ever seeing that. Jean, I want to take her out of my will. What will I have to go through to do it, cost-wise?

Jean: That's something you should talk through with your family lawyer.

Anne: I don't have a family lawyer! I asked you to be my shepherd because you're a lawyer!

Jean: Yes, Anne, I am a lawyer, but that's not what got us started, and I'm worried that my lawyering with you could get in the way of the other things that we've both said you're beginning to handle well after Joe's death.

Anne: All I want is advice on how to change my will. How could that affect things between us?

Jean: Maybe it wouldn't, but if I act as your lawyer, I'm not sure I could do something else that, as your shepherd, I think is important, too.

Anne: What's that?

Jean: Listening more. I think you've got a lot more talking to do about what all this anger may be about, and talking about it might help keep you from taking an action too soon that you might regret later.

Anne: (smiling) Some lawyer you are ...

Jean: How am I doing as a shepherd?

Anne: Great, darn it.

SOME QUESTIONS TO THINK ABOUT

1. What kinds of things do people often seek your opinions or advice about? How responsive are you to their requests? How much personal satisfaction do you get from sharing your opinions and advice with others?

2. How would you assess your gifts in the following areas of shepherding:
- guiding a care receiver toward a deeper devotional life;
- helping a care receiver to find and explore scriptural passages that speak to his or her life situation;
- sharing comfortably your faith and the difference it makes in your life;
- exploring with a care receiver what being a Christian can mean;
- encouraging a care receiver to discover new ways of serving others.

3. What do you understand to be the principal differences between being a consultant and being a shepherd?

14. Self-Disclosure: How Much Shall I Tell You about Me?

EARLIER IN THIS BOOK, WE EXAMINED THE BASIC CONDITIONS THAT make shepherding relationships possible. Maintaining these conditions is the most important responsibility of every caregiver who has any hope of helping others. We called upon shepherds to offer empathy, genuineness, respect, hopefulness, and affirmation, no matter what a care receiver may feel and think. These five gifts are bulwarks against the anxiety, impatience, self-doubts, unrealistic expectations, anger, guilt, and boredom that can weaken a shepherding relationship.

Can shepherds accomplish these things without disclosing more of themselves? If so, is it not their obligation to disclose more? Is the proper stance for shepherds, clergy and laity, one of neutrality and nonsharing of themselves while ministering to others? Can the outcome of caring acts be affected negatively by too much self-disclosure on the part of shepherds? These questions will form the framework of this chapter. The conviction to be put forward is that a high degree of self-disclosure is inescapable in shepherding relationships and is one of the distinguishing features of both pastoral counseling and lay shepherding. Such self-disclosure is one of the most important sources of their effectiveness.

ON THERAPIST ANONYMITY
For decades, therapists who followed in the psychoanalytic tradition made the couch the center of their offices and, as Freud did, positioned themselves

behind and out of view of their patients. They then invited their patients to pour out whatever came to mind, freed from all interruptions save those that were essential to the treatment. By such an approach, therapists came to know almost everything about their clients, but their clients were carefully shielded from learning almost anything about them. In retrospect, we can say that patients needed most the one thing that Freudian therapists most ardently withheld—a healthy relationship with a therapist known at a deep level in his or her humanness. Freudian therapy was in principle faceless, and as such, heartless.

To the chagrin of most Freudians who studied their master's work fully, Freud had an astonishingly mundane reason for seating himself out of his patients' view: he did not like to be stared at. Further, his case studies would reveal conspicuous violations of therapist anonymity had Freud subscribed to the principle. He was casual about treating friends and even relatives and about interacting with them outside the therapeutic hour. And he saw no impediment to his therapeutic relationships from the widespread fame that made anonymity impossible for him. Nowadays, psychoanalytically oriented practitioners take a far more personal approach to working with clients than classical doctrine allows, even if they remain cautious about too much self-disclosure with clients.

For most pastoral counselors, warnings against self-disclosure have come principally by way of Rogerian, client-centered therapy and its strong influence on pastoral care practice. For Rogers, therapy centers on the issues and concerns of the client. Because the therapist's task is to help the client see himself or herself more clearly and more appreciatively, only what is in the client is to be reflected to the client. Many standard therapeutic interventions such as evaluation, interpretation, and advice have to be strictly limited if not prohibited. Though Rogerian therapy is very much face to face, the therapist's face is in no sense to be a window to his or her soul. Rather, it is a means of communicating a sufficient degree of warmth, empathy, and unconditional positive regard to enable clients to dwell less anxiously on themselves and to look more eagerly within themselves for the healing resources they first request from their therapists. From such a standpoint, therefore, anything the therapist might disclose about himself or herself can only stand in the way of the client centeredness that is the touchstone of Rogerian therapy. The client and not the therapist must be the subject of the conversation at all times.

THE PASTOR'S DILEMMA

One of the most difficult adjustments that pastors and pastoral counselors in my generation have had to make in their respective ministries is to suffer the withdrawal pains of a seminary-induced addictive regard for Rogerian principles. Upon first encounter, client-centered therapy appears congruent with a Christian attitude toward others. It is relatively easily learned. It provides a wide safety margin against doing inadvertent harm to others. And it continues to have supporters throughout the mental health professions. Gradual recognition of its limited usefulness in pastoral situations, therefore, inevitably is accompanied by surprise, sadness, and even dismay. The recognition begins fairly early for most pastors. Most of the crises that shape their daily rounds require direct, active interventions of the sort prohibited by the nondirective counsel Rogerian therapy offers. The kind of withholding of self that Rogers called for is something that ministers, clergy or lay, soon find to be unmanageable, however commendable the principle may be in the abstract. Because the context for ministering is significantly different from that of psychotherapy, the nondisclosure that may be essential to a therapist's aim is often at odds with that of a minister.

As all pastors become aware, often painfully, they are subject to immediate and relentless scrutiny by all and sundry for the ways they do and do not perform their public, official functions and for the ways they do and do not live their lives in accordance with the expectations of their congregations and their communities. Their extensive and varied responsibilities—for preaching, leading worship, teaching, community involvement, organizational management, visitation in hospitals, nursing facilities, and homes, counseling, and the well being of their family members—make them visible to many different kinds of people who see them in many different lights. Inescapably, they must disclose more of themselves in the process of their ministry than they might want or even imagine.

Pastors are the subjects of countless questioning, second-guessing, anecdotes, testimonies, fantasies, criticisms, and idealizing, long before they have any opportunity to present themselves as the persons they are. Especially significant to the ways in which pastors come to be perceived is the fact that so many of their activities have a representative quality about them, in the fullest sense of what re-presenting signifies. That is, they bring to presence realities and powers that far transcend them—the congregation or judicatory that has ordained them, the community of Christians subsisting at all times and everywhere, the neighborhoods for whom their congregations have accepted at least some measure of responsibility, and God.

Not only do pastors disclose themselves in every moment of their daily activities, but also and in spite of themselves they become powerful screens for other people's projections. Because an encounter with a pastor is in a crucial sense an encounter with the One who has sent him or her, everything that is unresolved in anyone's relationship within himself or herself and with God will become grist for that person's experience of that pastor. By virtue of their own calling and others' perceptions of it, pastors represent God to people. Whatever perceptions, thoughts, and feelings people have about God will influence their perceptions, thoughts, and feelings about pastors, no matter how neutral any particular pastor may strive to be in projecting himself or herself.

Pastors always disclose something of themselves to those in their care, whether they want to or not. And insofar as any pastoral counselor goes about his or her own work with clients in a distinctively pastoral rather than merely clinical way, that counselor will face the same issues that pastors face when they find more of themselves already disclosed than they might like. This process is inescapable, and effectiveness in pastoral ministry depends heavily on whether or not pastors and pastoral counselors will claim the authority their office bestows upon them with both appropriate humility toward their shortcomings and with the confidence that God intends them to have in their ministry.

ANONYMITY NOT AN OPTION FOR SHEPHERDS

Contrary to what we might suppose, what has just been said about pastoral relationships fully applies to lay shepherding relationships as well. For those who may have doubts about this, let me offer several statements of care recipients that their shepherds have shared with me. The shepherds were dealing with a variety of feelings and thoughts that the statements evoked in them.

- *Sam, with all that you do around the church—I see your name on just about every committee we have—I can't believe that you're taking time to talk with someone like me. There are so many more important people in the church who must need you, I feel guilty taking up your time.*
- *When our pastor suggested assigning a lay shepherd to me, I was a little put out that he didn't seem to think my issues were worth the attention of anybody on the staff. And I really wondered how you could be of any help—we've taught together for years in the Sunday school and all. But you know, Trudy, you've become the most important person*

in my life, and I can't imagine what things will be like when we aren't talking like this together anymore.

- *I feel a very special bond with you. I can tell you things I would never tell anyone else—not my pastor, not my parents, not my husband, not anybody!*

- *The best thing that happened to me this past week was being in church on Sunday when you and Dorothy brought your baby to communion and put your hands over the pastor's when he blessed her. I just wanted to break down and cry, because I feel so cared about when I'm with you, but my faith is so much weaker than yours.*

Something deep and powerful has to be going on in shepherding relationships for these kinds of responses to emerge so spontaneously. Devotees of psychoanalytic thinking might suggest that such statements are troubling indicators of an idealization process that lay caregivers are ill equipped to handle. According to this kind of thinking, the shepherds have allowed an unwholesome dependency to develop that may sabotage their care recipients' spiritual growth. My view is that these statements reflect the depth dimension of all helping relationships in Christian contexts. People receiving care in such a context cannot help but project a great deal from their unconscious and the wellsprings of their spiritual striving as they come to know those who shepherd them. Good shepherds deal with the process by refocusing attention from themselves and to God as the vital center of every shepherding relationship. One shepherd dealt with the issue this way.

Rich: *When we started talking together, I never dreamed I would ever get out of the mess I had made of my life. But you made it happen for me. When I see you singing in the choir now, I say to myself, he really is God's man. I'm so thankful you've been here for me. What can I ever do for you that could even come close to what you've done for me?*
Shepherd: *Rich, when I pray about our work, I thank God for making me an instrument of his presence to you.*
Rich: *You're giving all the credit to God!*
Shepherd: *And to you!*

Throughout his ministering to Rich, this shepherd stayed alert to Rich's tendency to put him on a pedestal. He frequently made Rich's perceptions and misperceptions of himself an explicit issue in the shepherding relationship. With the help of his peer group, he decided that even more self-disclosure on his part would give Rich additional data against which he could check out more carefully his idealizing impressions. His next conversation included the following interchange:

Shepherd: *Rich, part of me would really like to accept your nomination of me to be God, but the other part knows that you really do know me better than that. I've struggled with the same thing you're struggling with now and don't have a complete handle on it even yet.*

Rich: *But you're a whole lot farther down the road than I am.*

Shepherd: *I don't know about "a whole lot," but I have learned a few things from hard knocks that you've said you've found helpful.*

Rich: *I guess we are more like fellow travelers on this, aren't we?*

Shepherd: *And God is right there on the road with us.*

ON NOT TAKING OURSELVES TOO SERIOUSLY

Like Rich, most of our care receivers at one time or another tend to make heroes and heroines of us, whether we are comfortable with the process or not. Sometimes we may get too comfortable with the adulation. Who among us does not like to be appreciated and praised? Rich's shepherd understood well what was going on and did not let himself get carried away. While showing respect for his care receiver's gratitude and deep regard, he wisely chose not to allow the proffered halo to attach itself to his head.

Another aspect of haloing needs to be mentioned. People who tend to be overly romantic, dramatic, sentimental, or glowing in their reactions to others usually have a problem with their self-image. They revere others too much because they think too little of themselves. And their inner fragility makes them especially vulnerable to disappointment when cherished others do not live up to their expectations of them. (They do not because they cannot. No one can.) Often the disappointment turns to anger and even rage at the person who had been idolized. Often the one now demonized is left to shake his or her head, wondering what happened. Another reason for helping care receivers to develop more realistic perceptions of us, therefore, is that by doing so we will decrease the likelihood that our imperfections and mistakes will provoke a care receiver to reject us and the help we can give.

For shepherding, the issue of self-disclosure as a means of helping people is the issue of exposure. It is especially the issue of making one's exposure a positive rather than negative force in ministering. The key to dealing with this issue is for shepherds to remain steadfast in their openness to the gospel message in their lives and at appropriate times to share that openness—with its struggles, triumphs, and joys—with those for whom they are called to care. This kind of self-disclosure is most fundamentally a bearing witness to the Christian gospel in all its challenge, demand, glory, and transforming power, and to how we are and are not living up to it.

How we listen for the claims of God upon our own lives is the most important kind of self-disclosure that any shepherd can offer to others. In this kind of self-disclosure, we acknowledge that we frequently fall short of our commitment to live as God desires us to live, and in this we are truly exposed for what and who we are. But we also bear witness to God's grace and forgiveness, grateful for the new possibilities God always opens to those whose hearts are truly penitent. In all of this, we share our care receivers' deepest spiritual struggles. Disclosures, in timely but not intrusive fashion, of ourselves as we truly are before God, are an indispensable part of all effective shepherding relationships.

SOME QUESTIONS TO THINK ABOUT

1. Think back on a time when you felt like you were bursting to share something with someone. Try to recall what you wanted to share, with whom and how you shared it, and what the response was. Can you see yourself now feeling the same way in a shepherding situation? What do you imagine you might want to say? Would you say it? Why or why not?
2. You are in the middle of a conversation with a care receiver who is struggling to maintain a hold on his faith during a particularly trying time. Suddenly he turns to you and asks plaintively, *What is Christian faith all about anyway? I'm not sure I know anymore.* What would you say?
3. Do you believe that there could be circumstances in which it might prove helpful for you to share some of your struggles and shortcomings?

15. Suggesting Tasks: Homework That Helps

GOOD SHEPHERDING CONSISTS LARGELY OF OUR BEING AVAILABLE, LISTENING well, remaining nonjudgmental, and resisting the impulse to fix things. Only rarely will we do things for our care receivers. Most of the time, we just sit there! We wait patiently for our care receivers to share with us what is on their minds and hearts. We struggle to understand better their distresses, hopes, and plans. We pray with them. Throughout, our primary goal is to help them decide for themselves what to do about their issues:

Well, Bill, there are a lot of things to think about here, aren't there?

Where do you think might be the best place to start?

Though there will be moments when we guide our care receivers, for the most part we follow them and with them listen for a fresh word from God about where God intends them to go.

Some situations, however, call for a more active stance on our part as shepherds. Some care receivers get so mired in their problems that they do not know where to begin working on them. Others generate a lot of energy and motion in their struggles but lament repeatedly that they aren't getting anywhere. Among the most difficult care receivers to deal with are those who love to talk with us—repeatedly—about the stresses and strains of their lives but resist action. These kinds of situations illustrate the appropriateness and even necessity of making specific suggestions to at least some of our care receivers, in the interest of overcoming their inertia and encouraging their growth:

> *I can't help thinking that what you need is to go and talk over with your brother and sister what they think the best care for your folks might be. You've been trying to make decisions about a big issue all by yourself, and you're completely stressed out over it. How about getting their input, and then let's talk the situation over in the light of what they offer?*

This chapter will explore the why, when, and how of suggesting specific tasks to care receivers as a way of helping them with their crises and with their growth.

I WANT TO GET BETTER, BUT ...

Shepherding is by no means the only context in which caregivers have to weigh constantly whether to continue listening to their care receivers or to encourage them to do something specific about their situation. For instance, most mental health professionals assume an active role in the therapies they provide, whether as a dispenser of medicines, a case manager, a surrogate parent, or an expert consultant. Listening to the client remains important. But the therapist also bears a major responsibility to determine what he or she will do for the client. Little value is ascribed to the client's becoming his or her own healer or to therapists who accept fees just to be "a very present help in time of need." With this proactive stance, therapists are unwilling to leave it up to their clients alone to work out the applications of their therapy.

Especially important is assigning tasks to be performed between sessions and careful monitoring of whether and how clients' homework was done as prescribed. Generally such assignments follow the form of sequencing the actions that must be taken eventually to resolve a problem and then asking clients to perform those actions one small step at a time. Success in completing the first of what will be many steps makes each succeeding step that much easier. Here, in the context of a shepherding rather than a therapeutic relationship, is an example of how a homework assignment helped a young woman find some of the energy she needed in order to deal with serious problems in her family.

Diane complains in tones of despair that the excitement has gone out of her relationship with her husband. When her shepherd, Betty, asks what they like to do together for fun, Diane responds plaintively that with three young children in the house and no one else available to take care of them, they have not been able to go out on a date for months, much less indulge the hobbies that brought them together. Betty is fully aware of the many difficult issues with which Diane and her husband are dealing constantly—conflicts with in-laws, financial difficulties, and parenting a child with Down's syndrome. She has been a good listener as Diane laid out each problem over several meetings. Tonight, though, Betty has chosen to take up a different stance with her care receiver. She encourages Diane to plan with her husband a night out and to report on how it went at their next session. Diane's reaction does not surprise her.

Diane: *It might be nice, but there's no way. We don't have money to do things like that right now, the kids need constant supervision, and though it's sad to have to say it, we aren't feeling very good about each other these days and we probably wouldn't enjoy it anyway.*

Betty: *You're saying you'd like to do it, but ...*

Diane: *But we just can't.*

Betty: *You want to, you don't think you can, and so you won't.*

Diane: *(irritated) Why is this such a big deal? With all we've got on our plates, you're telling me to just forget about it and go out and have fun!*

Betty: *I don't think you can or should forget about the things that you know you need to be working on. But I think that you are desperate to begin enjoying your marriage again.*

Diane: *(smiling) So, Doctor, this is your prescription for a better marriage?*

Betty: *I'm writing it out as we speak!*

Diane: *(sarcastically) Well, while you're doing that, maybe you can tell me just how and where I'm going to get it filled.*

Betty: *Right here! Let's see what has to happen to bring this off. What will you have to do first? And what will the next step be after that!*

Getting these questions answered satisfactorily did not prove easy, but Betty persisted and patiently guided Diane through the basics of arranging for a date, basics that she and her husband had lost sight of under the pressures they had allowed to build up in their relationship. Betty helped Diane rediscover how to have fun without spending much money, how to find a qualified sitter whom she could trust, and how to communicate with her children the appropriateness of Mommy and Daddy having a good time all by themselves. Most importantly, she elicited from Diane a commitment to follow through on her assignment and aroused in her an eagerness to make a report on it in the next session. The date was not a magical solution to all the other problems Diane had to deal with, nor were the dates that followed, pleasant as they were. Renewing the dating aspects of her marriage did help her to practice her improving communication skills, and by doing so to become more adept at coping with the more serious issues in the marriage.

Such assignments serve at least two valuable purposes. One is to help people consolidate and apply whatever learning they glean from their shepherding sessions so that the guidance they receive will produce longer-term benefits. The other is to assist the shepherd to uncover more of the underlying factors that may inhibit a care receiver's progress toward an agreed-upon goal. For instance, had Betty not given the homework, she might not have unearthed some valuable clues about how deeply troubled Diane's marriage was. Often, learning why a prescribed task was not completed satisfactorily or perhaps was not attempted is the most effective way of getting at the heart of a person's problem. And so, assigning and reviewing tasks, which is common to psychotherapy, is vital to Christian shepherding, too. Both faith without works and talk without action can deal death to the soul.

ACTIVE SHEPHERDING

However trendy assigning of tasks may be in psychotherapy, it is hardly a new thing to the shepherding of souls. By its nature, shepherding is action-oriented. Shepherds listen, observe, and reflect, but they also lead, guide, and intercede. However, they do not do these things because the standards of a professional guild require them to. They do them because they are called to represent the One who is the true shepherd and bishop of every human soul.

A capable shepherd will not hesitate to call another to become more responsible before God by taking specific kinds of actions to deal with whatever is getting in the way of their becoming the persons God intends for them to be. The key phrases here are "becoming more responsible before God" and "the persons God intends." Together they point to the kinds of task assignments that are distinctive to shepherding more than to therapy:

- praying more frequently and thoughtfully;
- forgiving those who have offended and even harmed us;
- engaging more consistently in both private and public worship of God;
- searching the Scriptures with greater diligence;
- fasting and other acts of self-denial; and
- expanding the breadth and depth of our acts of love toward others.

In the history of pastoral practice, these represent the most general kinds of tasks the Christian community has expected of its members on an ongoing basis. We call them means of grace, that is, ways of experiencing God's presence and love personally. The point is not that our performing one or more of these kinds of acts makes us worthy to receive God's grace. If this were true, then our salvation would depend upon our works rather than our faith. Instead, the point is that the grace that God already has bestowed upon us will become an experienced and not just a hoped-for reality to the extent that we make these revered means of grace increasingly important in our everyday living.

As shepherds, we have the responsibility to translate these general categories of grateful acts of obedience into terms specific to a distressed care receiver's situation. By doing so, our care receivers will have available more ways of allowing God's power and love to make the difference God intends for them to make. To this end, we might assign any number of tasks, such as

- complementing every prayer that requests something from God (petition) with a prayer of commitment to do God's will (submission);
- tangibly offering forgiveness to someone who has offended or even harmed our care receiver;
- meeting at church and for lunch together the next Sunday;
- reading some of the psalms that express the pain of loss or the sense of being abandoned by God;
- meditating on one or more passages from the Gospels that depict Jesus' obedient suffering;
- performing a genuinely sacrificial act for one's own benefit (e.g., fasting one day a week) or for someone else's (e.g., serving meals at a shelter for the homeless).

All of these examples represent specific kinds of invitations that individual shepherds make to individual care receivers in individual situations. They are not part of a general manual of interventions for every shepherd eventually to use with every care receiver in every kind of situation. Prayer, forgiveness, worship, and devotion, using the Scriptures, sacrificial acts, and works of love all are central in shepherding others in the name of Christ. And they help to differentiate Christian caring from therapy. But the role that each plays in a shepherding relationship will differ from person to person, requiring careful understanding and discernment on the shepherd's part.

Assignments based on the means of grace can be just as ill timed, inappropriate, and unhelpful as hastily thought out assignments of even the most competent therapists. Consider the following example of a poorly considered task assignment in the context of lay shepherding:

Tom: *Everything that I've worked hard for all my life is gone—my house, my family, my career, my health—you name it. I'm angry with* *myself, with the church, and even with God.*

Shepherd: *What you've got to do now, Tom, is to get down on your knees and just open your heart to the Lord. Say, our church's prayer support group is meeting tonight in the chapel. I'll pick you up, and we'll go together.*

Under other circumstances, with another care receiver, or even at a different time in Tom's life, an encouragement to pray might be the most helpful thing for a lay shepherd to do. In this case, it is not.

Tom: *I know you mean well, but that's the last thing in the world I could even think of doing right now. Maybe we'd just better put our talk on hold until I can figure out what I'm going to do with my life.*

Nor was the following task assignment:

Doris: *You're right, I have been looking tired lately. I am tired. Worn out, in fact. There are so many projects going on now at church that I'm involved in that I've been rushing, rushing, rushing trying to get things and people where they're supposed to be at the times they're supposed to be there, and it's been all I can do to keep up with it all.*

Shepherd: *Doris, it's just wonderful all that you are doing for so many people. You are truly an inspiration. Be sure, though, that you're keeping up with your Bible reading. The chapters in Luke that tell about Jesus' journey to Jerusalem could be especially important right now. I'd like for you read them for our next week's conversation. Okay?*

Doris: *(after a pause) I'll certainly try.*

Both vignettes illustrate how important it is that a shepherd's assignment of a task be relevant to the care receiver at the time. Because something worked for someone else at some other time does not mean that the person before us will benefit from it now. By God's grace, most of our mistakes in this regard will be overlooked by our care receivers, because they trust, as Tom did, that we mean well. But they can nevertheless have seriously detrimental consequences to our other efforts to be helpful during the interval it may take for care receivers to forgive our misstep.

The attention given in the previous paragraphs to decidedly spiritual tasks is not intended to suggest that these are the only kinds of tasks that shepherds consider in their ministering to people. Diane's shepherd, for instance, had no hesitation about assigning something that directly and emphatically addressed her need to play more and to learn again how to enjoy doing so. Nevertheless, there is an overarching perspective to all task assignments from a shepherding perspective, whether those assignments in themselves are worldly or spiritual. Their aim is to strengthen the other's relationship with God. Other tasks that a shepherd might assign—taking off for the weekend, visiting a parent in the nursing home, taking the children to the circus, making out an application, finding out where and when driver training is offered, cleaning a corner of one room of the house, giving away a deceased spouse's clothing—are far more likely to prove successful in a shepherding relationship when those who accept them are seeking also a renewal of their life with God.

SOME QUESTIONS TO THINK ABOUT

1. How comfortable are you with listening to someone in distress without offering any suggestions to them, making a strong recommendation of a specific action for the other to take, discovering that what you suggested did not work, and accepting the other person's refusal to do what you recommended?
2. What has been the most important application of the one-step-at-a-time principle in your life?
3. Of all the tasks that shepherds typically encourage those in their care to take up, which have been the easiest or most difficult in your spiritual life? On which do you think you are able to offer the greatest help? Why?
4. How would you invite a care receiver to take a particular step toward dealing with a problem in his or her life without your falling into a pattern of telling the person what to do or how to live?

16. Reframing: A Lot Depends on How You Look at It

SOME OF THE MOST DAUNTING CHALLENGES THAT COLLEGE AND graduate students confront have little to do with meeting the demands of unpredictable professors, fulfilling never fully understood degree requirements, or overcoming the anxiety accompanying the first day of the first job. In my case, these seemed almost inconsequential in comparison with the terror that broke into an otherwise placid existence when most of my fellow students and I confronted fast-approaching ends of months without the resources to pay our bills. Somehow we managed to do enough creative financing, with help from compassionate creditors, to survive for another month—and then another and another.

Occasional extravagances compounded our difficulties but also offered relief from the dreariness of never making ends meet. One such extravagance I remember fondly was the purchase of a print to add some beauty to a utilitarian dormitory room. When my roommate and I saw it in the art store window, we shared a stunned exclamation, remained transfixed for more than a few moments, and then noticed the little price tag hanging to the side. Neatly distinguishing the cost of the print from the cost of the frame, the tag made plain that what we saw was within our reach financially —but only if we bought the print and left behind the frame for someone wealthier than we were. But, as the store manager gently and rightly kept pointing out to us, sympathetic to our dilemma but enjoying the collective gleam in our eyes, it was the frame that made the print. We could not help but agree and delightedly plunged further into debt for the privilege of having available for constant viewing a stunningly mounted "Starry Night" by Vincent van Gogh. For nearly forty years I have been deeply grateful for my roommate's generosity in letting me take this beautifully framed print when we divided our collective purchases upon graduation. My wife and I continue to cherish Van Gogh's vision, which we have displayed in our little foyer.

Connoisseurs of art may find this vignette too precious for notice. While it may be possible to enhance an imitation of a great painting by external trappings, they might argue, the original is not more beautiful because someone has thought to mount it in a particularly attractive way. Starving seminarians, however, are unable to appreciate the subtlety of this observation, since they have no possibility of attaining the kind of access to the originals by means of which they could assess for themselves this delicate point of art criticism. But most seminarians at some time or other make their ways to the places where original works of art are available for everyone to see and discover there that curators devote considerable and loving attention to the ways in which even the greatest works are displayed. Here, too, just as in our small dormitory room, frames sometimes do make a painting. Whatever may be the so-called objective qualities of great paintings that demand appreciation on their own merits, our experiences of their beauty, and therefore of the meaning they will have for us, are shaped by the surroundings within which they appear to us: in short, by their frames. Often, reframing a painting creates it anew.

What is true for paintings is also true for the events we experience, the memories we hold, the plans and decisions we make, the people we know, the projects we undertake, the feelings we harbor, the thoughts we entertain, the actions we perform—and of the general shape of our life. What all these things look like, seem to be, mean, portend, hold, imply, suggest, depend in no small measure on what we make of them—on the kind of context, background, and setting we create for them, in essence on how we frame their appearance to us. As the same painting can take on a different significance when it is encased in a different frame, everything that affects our lives can assume a strikingly different value to us by our creating new settings in which they appear to us. All of the copies of the "Starry Night" print that my seminary roommate and I saw in the art store forty years ago were the same. But set in a wide frame painted in a midnight blue that caught and enhanced the grain of the frame's wood, my "Starry Night" continues to mean more to me than any copy of the print and even the original possibly could mean.

LOOKING AT THE PAST DIFFERENTLY

Childhood memories, by way of further example, may have the same constant features about them that photographs of remembered occasions have. And yet, arranged differently or viewed from a new vantage point, what both the memories and photographs mean can change dramatically. Clara's childhood memories were tinged with a longing and a sadness bordering on the morose. Her most powerful images were of an uncaring, emotionally distant, and physically absent father and of a mother always trying to explain and justify her husband as a good man. During conversations with Clara about her unhappy childhood, her shepherd suggested that she break out some family photographs before their next session and that they look at them together.

Three very old photos gave Clara something new to think about. One was of her father with a group of tired-looking, prematurely aged men ready to descend into a coal mine. Another showed him in a hospital room, surrounded by family members blowing out the candles on what appeared to be his birthday cake. A third showed Clara at about six or seven years of age on her smiling father's shoulders. Before this session was over, Clara had begun talking about her father as a man who worked himself to an early death trying to provide for his large family. Her shepherd commented on how interesting it was that while in one sense nothing about Clara's childhood changed objectively—"what was, just was"—in another sense everything about it might change if Clara continued to look at some things about it differently.

Sometimes a shepherd's major and perhaps only contribution to someone in distress may be by way of a timely suggestion to look at the same things from a slightly different perspective. This is particularly true when something about these things forever resists people's efforts to make them different than they are. Deprivation, neglect, abuse, losses, hostility, disappointments, frustrations, failures, illnesses, and tragedies—along with their opposites—contribute mightily to the texture of our lives, and they can no more be denied than can the basics of our distinctive anatomies. The frameworks we build around all these memories, however, are subject to reflection and choice.

As Clara discovered, it can make a tremendous difference which memories we allow to represent the whole of our experience across one or more periods of our lives. Did Clara's childhood consist of many unhappy times of longing for an absent father? Undoubtedly yes. Are the memories of those unhappy times to be regarded as conveying the substance of Clara's early life? Only Clara can decide. Her shepherd offered her a different way of valuing her childhood experiences by encouraging her to bring along some of the elements she would need in order to construct a new frame for her memories. When Clara allowed certain photographs to function as that new frame, all that her growing up had meant to her began suddenly and genuinely to change. In the words of Paul, old things began to pass away, and the new began to dawn *(2 Corinthians 5:17)*.

For Clara's mother, however, things were not so easy. Scornful of her daughter's newfound cheerfulness when attempting to commiserate with her about how things were, her mother continued to see only signs of misery in the family's sparsely filled photograph albums. She regarded Clara's attempted reframing of her experiences as naïve and silly. Many people would agree with Clara's mother. For them, looking on the bright side of everything serves only to blind us to the many harsh realities with which we have to deal. But human experience rarely adds up to a set of comforting illusions on one side starkly contrasted with a set of grim realities on the other, anymore than it does to a succession of negative misperceptions that constantly obscure the happy circumstances in which we live. To be sure, some experiences are incontestably good or bad in themselves, no matter how strongly anyone might perceive, want, think, or believe them to be otherwise. But whether the whole of our experience with other people, things, circumstances, and situations is good or bad is a different matter.

How our experience adds up is rarely determined by what happens to us as a result of external events and circumstances. What we make of it has to do primarily with our choice of which experiences of these external events and circumstances we will permit to represent the whole. We attend to some experiences more than we do to others. In her early family experiences, Clara, for instance, paid attention more to the meaning of her father's absence than she did to her mother's presence, which probably had a great deal to do with her mother's conspicuous lack of enthusiasm for her daughter's efforts at reworking her memories. As Clara's family chose not to cherish the memory of a birthday celebration in a hospital room, Clara gradually forgot about giddy playtimes with her father, depriving herself of a way to balance her memories of yearning for him during his absences and in spite of his seeming indifference.

One shepherd I know remembers vividly his struggles to help a fellow alcoholic, whom we will call Harry, get his life turned around. Harry had been drinking for so long that he had forgotten how it started. All he knew was that to his family he was a failure, a "falling-down drunk." Somehow, however, Harry managed to carry on with his addiction while keeping it away from work, and most of his fellow workers had an image of him as a good old boy who only once in a while went on benders. With tears in his eyes, Harry told his shepherd of his devastation when family members began cutting off contacts with him. With Harry's permission, his shepherd visited with two of Harry's aunts, who were his only family members living near by. He was surprised at what they told him. The aunts talked about Harry as a good man and good worker who years ago "took up the bottle" because he could not deal with the pain of being fired without cause from a job to which he had devoted all of his energy. One aunt said,

> *If I had had to put up with the things they did to Harry, I would have gone off the deep end a lot sooner than he did, and I wouldn't have climbed back up.*

Here is a brief portion of the conversation that followed between Harry and his shepherd:

Harry: *I haven't thought about that crummy time with — company in years and years. Everybody else in my family kept yelling at me that I got fired because of my drinking, and that's what I've thought, too.*

Shepherd: *So your aunt might have gotten it wrong?*

Harry: *You know, Aunt Bess was always the one person in the family everybody went to when they wanted to find out what was really going on with somebody else. No, she knew I'd been drinking a lot on and off the job then.*

Shepherd: *Do you think she's just making excuses for you?*

Harry: *Well, I sure do make a lot of excuses for myself. But she's right about my years on that job—I gave it everything I had, and it was never enough. I finally got passed over to make room for the boss's nephew, who didn't know diddly about how to do my job. I kept telling the boss that the bottom was dropping out, and sure enough it was. After they fired me, the company folded.*

Shepherd: *It interested me to hear her recollections about what you did after you were fired.*

Harry: *What do you mean?*

Shepherd: *She talked as if you climbed back up. But you've been sharing with me your feelings that you've stayed on the bottom. Could she be right?*

Harry: *I'd sure like to believe her.*

Shepherd: *Well, to me one sign that you might already believe her is that you and I are talking about your quitting drinking.*

Harry: *I guess I don't have to be a complete success at it to be a better man than I've been thinking I am.*

Shepherd: *Now, you're talking!*

Reconsidering our experiences from a new vantage point of greater maturity and wisdom is often a creation of experience anew. It does not deny so much as it transcends our history. We do not have to go on forever looking at things that have happened to us in the same way.

FACTS AND MEANINGS

Reframing does not suppose that the frame we construct to enclose and contain our experiences is the reality to be experienced. It only supposes that things that remain what they are by themselves take on different meanings for us when they are looked at, gathered, bounded, and set off differently. The invitation to reframe the meaning that people, events, circumstances, situations, experiences, and our reactions to them will have for us is not an invitation to play a game whose rules fantasy alone determines. Rather, it is an invitation to consider the possibility that old ways of looking at things may not be the most adequate ways of dealing with reality. As Paul wrote, our knowledge of things in this life is partial, but one day it will be whole, like God's knowledge of us now (1 Corinthians 13:12). From the faith perspective that is at the heart of all shepherding, reframing is one way of seeking to look at others and ourselves the way that God does.

For some people, such thinking can only provide the final and irrefutable warrant for concluding that reframing is mired in wishing for things that cannot ever be and that encouraging people to think this way only seduces them into not dealing with the real world. For is this not the sort of thing that religion has stood for across the millennia? No. Reframing does not deny the realities reframed, however strongly we might want those realities to be other than they are. And religion, far from denying unpleasant realities, seeks answers to questions about their existence sufficient to equip people to cope more effectively with them. The answers found in the religions of the world are powerful examples of what it can mean to reframe experience.

For the Christian tradition, God's definitive answer to all our questions about the mysteries of existence, including especially our questions about undeserved suffering, is to be found in the life, ministry, death, and resurrection of Jesus of Nazareth, confessed to be the Christ. As the Apostles' Creed expresses it, he "suffered under Pontius Pilate." For a moment, he earnestly hoped that his life would not end on a cross. "Father, if it be your will, take this cup from me." Then he turned his life, and every measure of his undeserved suffering, over to God. "Yet not my will but yours be done" (*Luke*

22:42, REB). Fully God, Jesus Christ was also fully human, and in him we find our own humanness, in the measure afforded us as finite, mortal beings fashioned from the dust of the earth.

If the heart of shepherding is guiding people's discovery of a vital faith and piety, then the reframing of our life issues in the light of the gospel message must remain a vital part of our ministering to others. For what else can that guidance be but a process of showing others how to view everything that they experience in reference to that message? Faith, as wholehearted trust in the Jesus who was and is confessed to be Christ, the preeminent manifestation of God's loving will for every human being, also is a way of seeing all experience in the light of that manifestation and that will. Because it is, a growing faith is a faith increasingly open to and familiar with looking at things in that particular way, however peculiar it may seem to others to do so. It is a way of continuing to seek out how God is working for good (*Romans* 8:28) in situations that provoke others to cry out "Curse God, and die!" (*Job* 2:9, REB); of accepting the future that God holds out to us even in the midst of bitter and grief-stricken sobs for children who are no more (*Matthew* 2:14, 18); of striving to see in all things signs of both the power and the goodness of that One who is our beginning and end; and of finding ourselves anew by losing more and more of our self-preoccupations in service with and to others.

SOME QUESTIONS TO THINK ABOUT

1. Think about a time when you made a deliberate decision to look at a situation in a new and different way. What was there about the situation that suggested doing this? What difference, if any, did your decision make to what happened subsequently?
2. When, in your judgment, is it helpful or harmful to insist that we keep looking on the bright side of things?
3. What to you is the difference between wishing for something, hoping for something, and seeing things as they are?
4. Paul wrote, "And we know that all things work together for good to them that love God, to them who are called according to his purpose" (*Romans* 8:28, KJV). What do you think this passage might imply to someone who has been fired from a job for no discernible reason; who lost everything she owned when a tornado tore through her trailer park; whose husband left her for another woman; whose three-year-old son has just died from leukemia?

17. Confrontation:
Facing the Truths That Hurt

S TANDING BEFORE KING DAVID, NATHAN THE PROPHET TOLD A HEART-
wrenching story about a rich man who shamelessly took for his own use
the only lamb of a poor man who had treasured and cared for it like a daughter. When David reacted with the expected outrage, Nathan promptly hurled
at his king one of the most famous confrontational phrases in the Bible: You
are that rich man. The parallel that the prophet drew by means of the story
was between the greed of one who needed nothing and a king's lust for the
wife of a loyal servant. Because David had violated Bathsheba and then sent
her husband Uriah to his death in battle, Nathan went on to warn of many
troubles that lay ahead for the king and his household (2 Samuel 12:11).

Central to this story's impact is the underlying assumption that only
someone speaking on behalf of God could presume to convey to a king the
depth of condemnation that Nathan's confrontation contained. This
assumption raises two particularly troublesome problems for us. The first
problem is with the notion of confrontation. Being confrontational often
suggests an aggressiveness that has come to seem out of place for Christians.
Once we could take for granted that discipline and reproof had an important place in Christian nurture. Nowadays, however, a live-and-let-live
philosophy has taken center stage, even in many of our churches. We dis-
parage people who take it upon themselves to speak for others, even when
we know that they are right to do so.

The second problem raised by Nathan's parable is its assumption, not that any of us may have to be confrontational at times, but that at least some of us may have to be confrontational on behalf of God. We live in a society enamored with individualism, pluralism, relativism, multiculturalism, the celebration of diversity, and the debunking of authority. In it, it is easy to become contemptuous of the remotest suggestion that someone might presume to pass judgment of any kind on anyone else's aspirations, inclinations, or actions. Who among us, the refrain now goes, could possibly claim to have a warrant to speak for God about anything? Human beings are the measure of all things! I (alone) am the captain of my own soul! Interestingly, however, we also bemoan the impending collapse of an each-to-his-own social order that discards social solidarity. And paradoxically, we offer grudging admiration to those we see as bold enough to impose their visions, plans, and will on others.

To these disparagements of confrontational and presumptuous people, however, another detail in the story of Nathan's challenge to David is especially cogent. That is David's acknowledgment: "I have sinned against the LORD" (2 Samuel 11:13). To bring the king to such an admission, Nathan unhesitatingly drew upon his divinely bestowed authority to speak words of judgment in God's name, to confront by the means of pronouncement. If, however, the passage represents a climactic moment in the encounter between a prophet and a king, as tradition holds that it does, then the three kinds of judgment of which the story speaks—Nathan's, God's, and David's self-judgment—are equally important to its outcome. We are accustomed to place the emphasis on the first two. But the third is of no less significance.

SEEING OURSELVES AS ANOTHER SEES US

As clear in its intent as Nathan's pointed comment to David might seem to be—and the story's impact depends upon our seeing its point immediately— "thou art the man" nevertheless and essentially is an invitation to its recipient to look at himself with eyes unclouded by the smoke of his vices and to consider anew what kind of a man he is. The demands of the story notwithstanding, David did not have to respond in the way that he did, with repentance and remorse. He might have responded in any number of other ways: "Who are you to speak of your king in such a manner?"; "What could that tall tale possibly have to do with me?"; "Bathsheba was no innocent daughter, and Uriah was no sweet lamb either"; "Kings can do anything they want." History is replete with chronicles of kings who lived by such morally reprehensible notions. But what David chose to do with

Nathan's confrontation was to take it in the spirit in which it was offered, as an invitation to self-reflection—specifically, on his professed faith, on his self-understanding as a man shaped by such faith, and on his behaviors toward Bathsheba and Uriah in the light of both.

In this case, the outcome was what the confronter had hoped for. Seeing the incongruity between his self-image and his actions, David chose to bring the latter back into line with the former. But choice was involved in making it so. Just as David could have refused to engage the confrontation, he could have chosen a different response to the self-reflection elicited by the confrontation: "After all, it is an honor for anyone to serve a king"; "Bathsheba wanted me as much as I wanted her"; "Uriah was in the wrong place at the wrong time"; "Who knows what the will of God is?" Such responses, and others equally self-serving, would have dissipated, at least for a time, any sense of the kind of inner incongruity in David that is intended to motivate all of us to change.

What makes this story so powerful is not only Nathan's exquisitely timed and executed confrontation but also David's passionately rendered response to it, which alone could bring about any real and lasting change in his kingship. As harsh and as seemingly aggressive as some confrontations may have to be in order to get their recipients' attention, their effectiveness has little to do with either the authority and power wielded by their users or the clarity and winsomeness of their own verbal content. Their effectiveness has everything to do with the willingness of their recipients to accept being called into question and to change for the better.

A LOVING BUT FORCEFUL INVITATION

In shepherding relationships, confronting another is not like angrily hurling a thunderbolt from a cloud-topped mountain to bring to bay a despised and frail mortal below, or haughtily driving terrified souls to their knees by verbal threats of everlasting punishment uttered righteously in the name of a furious Father, or decimating an enemy on the battlefield by an overwhelmingly superior force. It is a loving act, in the sense that it genuinely seeks the well being of the other and all those whose lives that other may affect. Here is how one shepherd confronted her diabetic care receiver after learning that she was not following her doctor's orders:

If you don't check yourself into the hospital for treatment right now, you're going to do more harm to yourself and maybe even to your children.

Confrontation is a forceful act, too. It deliberately strives to put unpleasant facts before another in a way that makes their avoidance or their evasion as difficult as possible.

You know, I've been listening to you for quite a while now speak with a lot of admiration and tenderness about your parents, and yet you also say that you haven't visited them in years and can't remember the last time you wrote or telephoned them.

But confrontation is an act of invitation whose outcome is more in the hands of the recipient than of the confronter.

What do you make of the fact that you aren't living up to any part of your agreement with her?

It might be tempting for an impatient or weary shepherd to tell a wayward care receiver merely that he or she is wayward. But if shepherds succumb to this temptation, they end up simply pronouncing judgment, judgment of a kind that almost certainly would bring their effectiveness as a shepherd to an end. Confrontation, as we are looking at it, is not passing judgment. Only God can judge. What shepherds can do, with a love that genuinely seeks others' well being before God, is to help those others see the incongruities in their beliefs, commitments, and actions and to communicate support for their every effort to bring their lives into conformity with God's will.

WHY WE FIND IT HARD TO CONFRONT

This characterization of confrontation as loving, forceful, and inviting may help to shed light on why it can be difficult to make constructive use of confrontation in the shepherding process, as well as on why confrontations sometimes fail. Let's take the characterizations in reverse order, beginning with the aspect of invitation. It is easy to tell someone what we think is wrong with them. It is more difficult to invite that person to deal honestly with himself or herself.

Confrontations often miss their mark because those who employ them do so more for the purpose of controlling outcomes on their own terms than for inviting another to make changes on his or hers. Sometimes even the right words can become instruments of controlling:

You say that you are worried about getting into heaven and that getting the abortion will anger God, and yet you aren't considering any other options for your pregnancy.

The shepherd who delivered these words was repelled by her care receiver's value system, attitude, and contemplated action and conveyed by the tone of her words and accompanying gestures a condemning judgment designed to shame the care receiver into carrying the baby to term and permitting adoption. At a purely verbal level, the statement looks like an invitation to reflection on alternatives. But what was meant and heard was

A faithful believer such as yourself obviously should not even be considering the possibility of abortion.

Such a statement obscures other alternatives that a competently rendered confrontation should open up, however unpleasing those alternatives are to the shepherd. For instance, the shepherd could have said, "God is a loving as well as an angry God," or "Abortion may not be an unforgivable sin." Confrontations are powerful instruments for helping people overcome incongruities in their thoughts, feelings, and actions, but only if those who make use of them are willing and able to tolerate resolutions different from their own.

The kind of inviting that makes for a confrontation has a forceful quality about it. It is not to be ignored. Some people who think of themselves as capable shepherds nevertheless fail those to whom they minister because of their unwillingness or inability to be forceful enough in the face of real threats to another's well-being:

Harry: *I lost a lot of sleep last night. My son didn't get me out of jail until almost two A.M.*

Shepherd: *You were in jail? For goodness sake, what happened?*

Harry: *Oh you know these office Christmas parties—I had a little too much to drink, I guess, and they stopped me for weaving across my lane toward the traffic coming from the other way. But I saw the cars and was getting back in my own lane. I don't know why they got so high and mighty with me.*

Shepherd: *(after some hesitation) It must have been irritating, getting stopped that way.*

At least we can say that this shepherd was empathetic. But empathy is not what was called for. A forceful though nonjudgmental confrontation might have gone this way:

Shepherd: *Harry, what on earth were you thinking of, driving home after all you'd been drinking? Have I been misunderstanding you after all? All you've been telling me about how sorry you are for the harm your drinking has caused people?*

For some shepherds, the failure to be forceful comes from their immaturity in dealing with challenges in their own lives, especially challenges their care receivers also may avoid or evade. It became clear in peer supervision, for instance, Harry's shepherd had a drinking problem and was not as far along in dealing with it as his fellow lay shepherds had believed he was. It is difficult to be confrontational with someone else when one is rarely, if ever, confrontational with oneself.

For other shepherds, the failure to confront forcefully comes from confusion between confrontation and judgment, combined with a specious interpretation of Jesus' words, "Judge not lest ye be judged" (*Matthew 7:1, KJV*). Shepherds mired in such misconceptions inadvertently join ranks with the multitudes in our culture who remain content to live their lives in a moral vacuum, rationalizing their self-pursuits with "Who am I to pass judgment on anybody else?" Confrontation is at times intrusive. Its aim is to break through another's naiveté, evasiveness, and irresponsibility. But confrontation is not by itself judgmental. Its primary aim is to help people to see more clearly the inconsistencies between their behavior and their professed values and to encourage them become their own judges.

Finally, difficulties with confrontation can express an inadequate understanding and/or practice of love. For example, some people cling naïvely to the prevailing view of love as a blissful feeling between people to be sought, savored, and protected at all costs. Holding such a view will hinder our confronting another when the other needs to be confronted. We may rationalize our failure to act in terms of our not wanting to upset the other. Or we may tell ourselves that we do not want to put the harmony in a relationship in jeopardy. But Christian love is not a superficial promotion of good feelings between everybody. It is a commitment to others' well being, notwithstanding the pain that such a commitment may bring about on the way to our realizing its proper goal.

It took a lot of energy, patience, compassion, and persistent love on the part of Harry's shepherd to help him to confront his failings with uncompromising honesty and develop a commitment to change. The vignette quoted went on:

Shepherd: *Harry, what on earth were you thinking of, driving home after all you had been drinking? Have I been misunderstanding you after all? All you've been telling me about how sorry you are for the harm your drinking has caused people?*

Harry: *You sound just like my wife! She read me the riot act, too, when I got home.*

Shepherd: *I don't know what your wife said to you. What I'm concerned about is that the bad feelings you have about your drinking don't*

jibe with the way you're handling the problem.
Harry: *You're calling me a liar?*
Shepherd: *Harry, you've been saying one thing and doing another. Is that lying?*
Harry: *I guess in a way it is. I've been lying to myself.*
Shepherd: *What do you want to do about that?*
Harry: *What do you mean?*
Shepherd: *Well, I think you've got three options: you can go on doing just what you're doing, you can go with your feelings of regret and remorse and give up the drinking, or you can keep drinking and stop telling yourself to feel so bad about it.*
Harry: *Well, what are you telling me to do?*
Shepherd: *I'm telling you to be honest with yourself.*
Harry: *I was afraid you were going to say that.*

CONFRONTATION WITHOUT JUDGMENT

Harry's shepherd just kept at it! But he did it nonjudgmentally. This does not mean that he had no opinion about what would be in Harry's best interest. On the contrary, because he felt so passionately about what would help, he held on tenaciously through Harry's many attempts at avoidance. The basis of his confrontations, however, was not his opinions but Harry's self assessment. When this shepherd pushed, he pushed Harry into the inconsistencies between his own words and actions, invited Harry to judge himself from within, and then with love supported Harry's entering an alcoholism treatment program. Because Harry accepted the invitation his shepherd's confrontation opened to him, he got well. With David of old, he chose the better course.

SOME QUESTIONS TO THINK ABOUT

1. How hard are you on yourself? hard enough? too hard? too easy? What helps you keep a good balance between healthy self-criticism and neurotic self-blame?

2. Have you ever been confronted by another's effort at discipline or reproof? Was the confrontation fair to you? Why or why not? How did you respond?

3. How easy or difficult is it for you to bring to someone else's attention what you think they need to look at in themselves? What helps you to do this effectively?

18. Becoming Partners in Prayer

We can approach God with this confidence: if we make requests
which accord with his will, he listens to us; and if we know that
our requests are heard, we also know that all we ask of him is ours.
(1 John 5:14-15, REB)

TWO OF THE MOST BEAUTIFUL PHRASES IN CHRISTIAN HISTORY ARE "FRIEND
in Christ" and "soul friend." From the standpoint of our faith, they
express what caring people are like at their best. A friend in Christ is someone who follows the example of Jesus even to the point of being willing to
sacrifice his or her life for another. A soul friend is someone who listens
patiently and compassionately to another's confessions. These characterizations apply well to shepherds. In both senses of the word friend, a shepherd is truly a friend to another.

There is still another sense in which the word friend describes Christian
shepherds. Friends in Christ, soul friends, and shepherds PRAY. Shepherds
pray for those in their care, they pray for one another, and they pray for
guidance and strength in all their caring. They invite their care receivers to
pray more openly and more constantly. And their prayerful attitude makes
them sensitive to and receptive of the prayers that others offer to and for
them. A shepherding relationship is a partnership in prayer, and the deep
friendship that often develops from it is anchored by the quality and depth
of the praying between the partners.

The purpose of this chapter is to explore prayer as a distinctively Christian component in the kind of caring that lay shepherds offer to others. We will attempt to answer three questions that all of us struggle with as we build prayer partnerships: What is prayer? How should we pray? How can we help our care receivers experience more deeply the power of prayer in their lives?

THE WHAT AND THE HOW OF PRAYER

For answers to the first two questions, we turn to two passages in the Gospels that contain the core of what our Lord had to say about prayer. Because they are so familiar to us from the King James Version, the texts are presented here in that translation. The first is from Matthew's Gospel, and the second is from Luke's. In Matthew 6:9-13 (KJV), Jesus' words about prayer are relayed in the context of a larger body of teaching imparted to a crowd of people early in his ministry in Galilee:

After this manner therefore pray ye:
Our Father which art in heaven,
Hallowed be thy name.
Thy kingdom come.
Thy will be done in earth, as it is in heaven.
Give us this day our daily bread.
And forgive us our debts, as we forgive our debtors.
And lead us not into temptation, but deliver us from evil:
For thine is the kingdom, and the power, and the glory, for ever.
Amen.

Luke's Gospel gives us a little different version of the prayer, and he places it in a different context. At Luke 11:2-4 (KJV), the prayer is as follows:

Our Father which art in heaven,
Hallowed be thy name.
Thy kingdom come. Thy will be done, as in heaven, so in earth.
Give us day by day our daily bread.
And forgive us our sins; for we also forgive every one that is
indebted to us.
And lead us not into temptation, but deliver us from evil.

In the scene that Luke describes for the prayer, Jesus is not teaching a large crowd. Instead, he is praying alone. He is observed by one of his disciples, who then asks him to teach all of them about prayer. Rather than at the beginning of his ministry in Galilee, Jesus speaks about prayer near its end, on the road to Jerusalem.

From the first century to the present, the Christian community has been of one mind that the two passages from the Gospels are the first and final word on prayer for Christians. In them, we, with Christians at all times and everywhere, discover what we need to know about the subject, for the sake of both our relationship with God and our ministry to others. Therefore, whatever differences we find between Matthew's and Luke's presentations of Jesus' words must remain inconsequential for the life of faith. For all of their many diversities, both Matthew and Luke were included in the one New Testament and with them, their two versions of one vitally important prayer. Just as both Gospels are necessary for our faith, both versions of the Lord's Prayer are necessary for our prayer life.

As we take our first close look at Jesus' words on prayer, one thing becomes apparent immediately. It is that questions about the what and the how of prayer are hard to distinguish with any precision. In Matthew's Gospel Jesus seems to emphasize more the how than the what ("This is how you should pray ... "). But the way he does it is interesting. He tells people what to pray! It is the same in Luke's version. There, Jesus first meets his disciples' request to be taught to pray by telling them what they ought to say in prayer. Is the Lord's Prayer by itself, then, to be taken as the sole expression of prayer? Is it all that we and our care receivers are to say in our prayers? This can hardly be what Jesus meant, since he is reported in the Gospels as saying all kinds of other things in prayer. What does he mean by the example that he gave? The answer of the Christian tradition is that Jesus means this particular prayer to convey everything that should go into all of our other prayers at one time or another. It also conveys a clear starting point for every prayer: God.

Prayer is centering on God: on God's supremacy, God's holiness, God's presence, God's will, God's sustenance, God's grace, God's protectiveness, God's salvation—on God who is the Alpha and the Omega, the First and the Last, the Beginning and the End. In our praying, we center on God in an attitude of awe, respect, adoration, yearning, praise, thanksgiving, humility, and commitment. And we let our words and our silences glorify him as the only source and end of our existence and our joy, who alone is the proper object of unconditional love, loyalty, obedience, and service, forever. Our Father ... the kingdom, and the power, and the glory are yours, forever and ever ... thanks be to God.

We begin to fathom the depths of prayer when it dawns on us for the first time that we can never say all that we want to say about God—to God.

Paradoxically, in some of our deepest moments of prayerfulness (prayer-fullness) it can seem to us that we do not know how we ought to pray. We may grope for words, stammer only some of them out, moan, or fall even more deeply into silence before God's power, wisdom, goodness, and glory. It will not matter how many words we may have at our disposal for every other purpose. When God graciously draws near to us, we will never have enough words to say to him what will be in our hearts. It will not matter that we are eloquent or that we lack eloquence; before God, our sighs will be too deep for words (*Romans 8:26-28*).

Sooner or later, though, words come, because they must. For our lives dwell eternally in the Word by whom all things were created, and by means of words we cry out the joy that is otherwise unspeakable, "Thou art my Lord, my God." We cannot help ourselves. We must pray. Often, though, the words we use are swallowed up in the wonder of bearing such a resemblance to our Creator that we can talk with God and God with us. Here are some of the words that faithful people use to tell God how overwhelmed they feel in his awesome, gracious presence:

> *I just want to keep on praising my God;*
> *I wish I had the words our preacher does to tell you how I feel about you;*
> *God ... God ... God ... God ... God ... God — lots of times,*
> *that's all I want to say;*
> *Thank you, thank you, thank you;*
> *Yes, yes, yes, yes, Lord;*
> *Amen, amen, amen ...*

If we were to compare prayers like these with some of the prayers of our tradition, we might be tempted to think that they do not measure up. We dare not succumb to this temptation. All of the prayers quoted express the spiritual depths of people who want to be honest in their relationship with God. There are no performance or eloquence tests in the life of prayer. All that God asks of us is that we approach him "just as we are." As one shepherd said:

> *The best thing that ever happened to me in my praying was when I discovered that I don't have to know all the time what to say to God. In fact, I don't have to say anything. It's okay to be still and listen. And sometimes, it's like God is telling me what to say.*

In English translations of the Lord's Prayer, the first reference to God is as Father. Most early readers of the Greek texts understood the fatherhood of God as having to do with God's awesome majesty, holiness, power, and sovereignty. God is our heavenly Father. Only God's will is everywhere to be done. Only God can protect us. Only God can forgive our sins (our "debts" or "trespasses"). And only God's kingdom deserves our loyalty and our hope. This is the Father whom we are to praise with every fiber of our being, in our waking and in our sleeping. "Father, I adore you, lay my life before you."

From praise and adoration of God, prayer flows naturally into thanksgiving. Early in our spiritual development, we focus our thanks on specific blessings. We give thanks for the meal before us, for nourishing rains and a plentiful harvest, for recovery from an illness, for our church's successful financial campaign—for just about any tangible benefit to us and to those who matter to us. Later, if our faith grows, our thanksgiving will well up from a deep and abiding sense of the gloriousness of all of God's works, everywhere. In the end, thanksgiving flows effortlessly into the adoration from which it originally springs. Just as all life begins and ends in God, so does all prayer. Gloria in excelsis deo! Glory to God in the highest!

Or, as Wanda prayed for herself and her shepherd:

Holy God, Father, we love you. Our lives are in your hands, and we are grateful. We trust you. Help us to seek your will for us in everything.

AN ILLUSTRATION

Wanda and her shepherd, Katie, have been through a lot together. The relationship began when Wanda started radiation treatments and chemotherapy for cancer. Frightened, she relied heavily on the soothing and strengthening presence of Katie, a cancer survivor herself. When her treatments proved to be unsuccessful, Wanda first blamed God for letting her down, and she refused Katie's offers to pray during their sessions. Katie accepted the refusals but told Wanda that she would continue praying for her on her own. *A lot of good that'll do,* Wanda spat out. Over the next months, the two spent many hours struggling together to reconcile Wanda's increasing pain with what their faith told them about a loving God. Wanda's anger gradually changed into sadness over the immense distance she felt between herself and God. At a particularly intense time of suffering and hopelessness, she said poignantly to Katie, *If there is a God at all, he must be too holy to care about people like us.*

From the depths of a spiritual crisis as searing to her soul as her cancer is to her body, Wanda cries out the kind of despair that afflicted so many in Jesus' lifetime: the despair over a too distant God who demanded too much and gave too little, a God too heavenly to pay attention to our earthbound needs and heartfelt requests. Was this distant God the God to whom our

Lord prayed? Is this the God to whom Jesus taught us to pray? Many people have thought so, including Wanda. And there are times, Katie confessed to her fellow shepherds, that she herself wonders what God may really be like. There is more, however, to Jesus' teaching about prayer and to Wanda's struggle with her faith, as we shall see. The next paragraphs offer a closer look at what our Lord's teaching says to us about becoming partners in prayer with our care receivers. The chapter will conclude with a brief discussion of what Wanda can teach us about trust, prayer, and the peace that passes all understanding.

As Matthew and Mark tell it, there was at least one moment in Jesus' life when he was overcome with that sense of estrangement from God that Wanda felt. On the cross, he cried, "My God, my God, why have you forsaken me?" (John Calvin wrote that this represented the moment of Jesus' true descent into hell.) But throughout his ministry, Jesus showed his followers a different side of God than this, a God who is always near, who cares about us, who listens and responds to us, who suffers with us, and who transforms our suffering. Blessedness, in this life and in the next, is the inheritance of all who suffer and die trusting with their whole being in him.

The most important clue that Jesus gives to this other side of God is contained in the very prayer that we have been considering. Jesus almost certainly offered the prayer to his disciples in the language that he and they spoke together, Aramaic. In that language, the word we translate as "Father" is *Abba*. It is a term of familiar, tender, intimate address from an almost childlike attitude. What comes closest to it in English is Daddy. Abba, Jesus tells his disciples, solicits, listens to, and responds to our prayers, personally and faithfully. Abba calls us to pray for ourselves (petition) and for others (intercession) honestly and constantly, in the confidence that he will respond.

To Jews burdened with a sense of obligation to fulfill an impossibly large number of barely comprehensible laws imposed by a glaringly absent but punitive sovereign over the universe, Jesus' message of an available, gracious, merciful, loving God must have seemed too good to be true. In this case, however, the too good to be true was true. It still is—for us, for our care receivers, and for every one of God's creatures everywhere.

The God whom Jesus addressed in prayer is none other than our heavenly Father, whose holiness and graciousness deserve our utmost and unqualified devotion and gratitude. What our Lord wanted his disciples especially to understand, though, is that God is also a present and loving Creator who takes our expressions of need with utter seriousness. To this God, we also can bring our confessions of sin, not from a terror that unless we do, he will destroy us, but from a confidence that what he most wants is to forgive and protect us. Finally, Jesus' God is the One to whom we can submit our wills unreservedly, because he is the most holy One who alone is worthy of our ultimate commitment and service.

The Lord's Prayer makes plain that Jesus wants his followers to comprehend the fullness of God. And what is that fullness? It is the unity of God's supreme holiness and God's loving concern for everything in all creation. Jesus' prayer expresses his comprehension of that fullness simply and eloquently. He asks us to do the same in our prayers.

HELPING OUR CARE RECEIVERS TO PRAY

To this point in this chapter, we have dealt with the first two of the three questions about prayer that we identified. By examining the context and the content of the Lord's Prayer, we have made a beginning in clarifying what prayer is and how we are to pray. Now we move to the third question: How can we help our care receivers to experience more deeply the power of prayer in their own lives? The answer is by practicing all of the kinds of prayers that Jesus' prayer illustrates so concretely.

Praising God from the depths of our souls:
   "Hallowed be thy name"
Giving thanks with grateful hearts:
   "For thine is the kingdom, and the power, and the glory, for ever"
Confessing our sins and shortcomings honestly:
   "Forgive us our debts"
Asking God to protect us:
   "Deliver us from evil"
Asking God to help us with our needs:
   "Give us this day our daily bread"
Asking God to make us instruments of help to others:
   "As we forgive our debtors"
Submitting our wills to God's will:
   "For thine is the kingdom, and the power, and the glory, forever. Amen."

Through incorporating all of these acts of praying we draw closer to God. This point cannot be emphasized too strongly. Prayer is adoration and thanksgiving and confession and petition and intercession and submission, addressed to God "without ceasing." It is not the practice of one or more at the expense of the others. To be sure, God is not asking that we pray all of these prayers each and every time we open our hearts to him. God is asking of us, however, that we become comfortable enough with them to include each of them at some time in our praying. In general, we will be comfortable praying them with our care receivers when we become comfortable with them in our own prayer life.

Frequently I ask lay shepherds about the kinds of prayers that tend to be prominent in their individual shepherding relationships. They consistently report that they and their care receivers do a lot of asking. This is as it should be. Both Matthew and Luke report Jesus' encouragement to his followers to approach God in just this way: "Ask, and you shall receive." Their point seems to be that unless we ask, it is less likely that we will receive!

The problem comes when we focus so much on petition and intercession that other ways of prayerfully expressing our trust in God are paid little more than lip service or are disregarded. Then prayer becomes little more than cajoling God to do things that he might not otherwise do. If we approach God this way, we can only oscillate between fear that we may not have found the right way to get through to God and resentment when our prayers do not bring about the results that we feel they deserve. Honoring and thanking God, confessing our sins, and committing ourselves to God's loving and everlasting care also are important expressions of our faith. When we engage in them regularly through our prayers, the desperate urgency that accompanies so many requests to God can become instead a serenity that knows God always will give us what we most genuinely need. Our primary task as their prayer partners is to help our care receivers to open themselves in every way to God and to express that openness more frequently in their praying.

RETURNING TO WANDA AND KATE

Wanda is dying, in spite of the fact that she and Katie have prayed sincerely to God for healing, over a long period of time. During her struggle Wanda becomes angry with God for not answering her prayers. Toward the end, she falls into a deep despair over feeling abandoned by God. By this time Katie feels that her own faith is being sorely tested, too. One night, as she returns home from the hospital after a particularly difficult conversation with Wanda, Katie prays silently some of Jesus' words in the garden of Gethsemene:

Father, not my will, but yours. Help me to accept it with love. Not my will ... yours ... yours ... yours ... I love you ... your will, not mine ... yours ... yours ...

Suddenly Katie feels led to return to Wanda's hospital room, where she finds Wanda in a deep sleep. She sits quietly by Wanda's bed for a while. After praying softly to Wanda the prayer she earlier prayed silently to herself, she goes home.

The next morning, Katie finds Wanda sitting up in bed, reading her Bible for the first time in many days. Looking at Katie with as much of a smile on her face as she could muster through her pain, Wanda says:

> I don't know why, Katie, but when I woke up this morning, the sadness didn't fall in on me like it's been doing to me.

Katie: *What a welcome relief! What did you feel instead?*

Wanda: *It's kind of hard to describe. I guess it was like a peacefulness that I haven't felt in a long time. (Wanda winces in pain.)*

Katie: *Even though you're still hurting a lot, you also felt peace.*

Wanda: *Yes, and I'm still feeling both right now. (following a long pause) Katie, I started praying this morning—can you believe it?*

Katie: *Care to tell me about it?*

Wanda: *I started thanking God for everything he has done for me instead of blaming him for what he hasn't. And then—now you're really going to think I've gone around the bend—I started crying—and crying—and crying—about all the bad things I've said about him. And at the end, I felt forgiven! And loved.*

Katie: *There's a sweet expression on your face—you're still feeling that love.*

Wanda: *From God and from you. I've been pretty rotten to you, too, haven't I? And you've just kept coming back and loving me.*

Katie: *I do love you, Wanda, and I know that God loves you too.*

Wanda: *I'd like for us to pray together right now, like we used to.*

Katie: *Would you like to go first?*

Wanda: *Yes!*

Wanda offers the prayer reported earlier in this chapter:

> Holy God, Father, we love you. Our lives are in your hands, and we are grateful. We trust you. Help us to seek your will for us in everything.

Late that afternoon, while Katie is struggling desperately through rush-hour traffic to get back to her in time, Wanda dies. Katie learns Wanda's last words through one of the nurses:

> Tell Katie good-bye for me, and that I love her, and that I'm going to be all right, now.

Katie is going to be all right, too.

SOME QUESTIONS TO THINK ABOUT

1. Recall as clearly as you can the prayers you have prayed this past week or so, in whatever context and on whatever occasion. What themes stand out particularly strongly: praising God, making requests, giving thanks? Would you say that these prayers are typical of those you usually offer?

2. What have been your most important experiences of knowing that someone else is praying for you? How have others' prayers enriched your own spiritual life?

3. How comfortable are you with praying in the presence of, or for, others?

4. What is your present understanding of how prayer is answered? Have you always believed this way? If so, who and what were the principal influences on the development of your beliefs about prayer? If not, how and why have those beliefs changed?

19. The Uses and Misuses of the Scriptures in Shepherding

AS WE AGE, MOST OF US FIND OUR VISION NEEDS CORRECTION. THINGS that we used to see distinctly become blurred. Sometimes we may have difficulty seeing them at all. We are fortunate when a well-fitted pair of eyeglasses turns out to be all we need in order to see clearly again. With the help of one of Protestantism's greatest theologians, John Calvin, we can discern in this rather mundane fact of life the basis of a profound spiritual truth: As our eyes sometimes need glasses through which to see the things of this world, our souls always need the Scriptures through which to see the workings of God.

Calvin's magnificent image of the Scriptures as lenses suggests that reading the Bible is like looking at the world and ourselves through God-colored glasses. If we keep the glasses on long enough, nothing will ever look the same again. Studying the Bible, we could go on to say, is like keeping a favorite pair of eyeglasses free of dust and polished to a sparkle, not so that we can fix our gaze admiringly on the glasses themselves but so that we can see everything else better through them.

TWO WAYS TO USE THE BIBLE

This chapter seeks to apply Calvin's comparison between the Scriptures and lenses to using the Bible in shepherding relationships. The primary application of the image will be to clarify the difference between looking at the Bible as an end in itself and looking with and through the Bible for a deeper understanding of our care receivers and their situations from God's point of view.

The first way leads mostly to misuses of the Scriptures. Its side roads detour through our churches as people debate, heatedly and usually uncharitably, the nature of biblical authority and the proper interpretation of the Scriptures. Whose position is the correct one: the liberals', conservatives', fundamentalists', charismatics', Marxists', feminists', deconstructionists', comparative religionists'? Each group, and others besides, will try to quiz us to see if we are on the correct side. For the purposes of shepherding, these squabbles will not get us far. Staying in the debates is like endlessly polishing our bifocals (or trifocals) without ever putting them on to see other things better.

The second way—looking at things by means of the Bible rather than looking at the Bible itself—is the more promising way. This way focuses not on what we should think about the Bible in theory but on how we should think about our care receivers' experiences as they are shared with us. It encourages a mutual exploration, between our care receivers and ourselves, of what those experiences might look like if they are seen in the light of what the Bible says about God's will for us as revealed in the life, ministry, death, and resurrection of Jesus Christ. It leaves us not with doctrines about biblical authority, or with definitive answers to our care receivers' dilemmas, but with a mutual openness to hear a fresh word from God at God's good pleasure.

LOOKING AT CONTEXT

Overcome with emotion, Laura could only sob. Words would come later. Her shepherd, Sharon, waited patiently, holding Laura's hand.

Laura: (trembling) I keep asking myself why Rob quit loving me ... I know I haven't been a perfect wife, but I've given him everything I have to give ... I keep thinking that it must be my fault, but I know I don't deserve the contempt I've gotten from him for so long ... the drunkenness ... and now the hitting. I just don't think I can take it any more. But God says I have to! I'm so scared! (Now Laura is shaking.)

Sharon: (putting her arm around Laura's shoulder) You are scared, Laura, more than I've seen you before.

Laura: I'm terrified.

Sharon: (holding Laura) Can you put words to what's terrifying you so?

Laura: It's what Mom keeps on saying. She's sure that if I leave Rob, I'll be committing a horrible sin and will be condemned by God.

Sharon: Does she give you reasons for saying that?

Laura: It's right in the Bible, Sharon, there's no getting away from it. Look! (Laura hands Sharon her Bible, opened to Mark 10:9) "What *therefore God hath joined together, let not man put asunder." What could be plainer than that? Right now I feel guilty for even thinking what I've been thinking about Rob and me.*

Sharon: *I read somewhere in the Bible that a husband should love his wife like Jesus loved his church.*

Laura: *That's in Ephesians, Sharon. But it doesn't give me the right to divorce Rob. I'm trapped, forever. If I stay with Rob, I'll be living in hell, and ... (long pause)*

Sharon: *... and if you leave, you're afraid you may go to hell.*

To this point in her shepherding, Sharon is listening well to her distraught care receiver, striving to understand better the place to which Laura had come in her struggle with a marriage that is failing. Only once does Sharon try to steer the conversation in another direction—toward a Bible verse that she hopes Laura might put alongside the one that disturbs her so. When Laura resists, Sharon returns to the listening, clarifying stance that won Laura's trust. But now, Sharon reports to her peer group, she said something that almost got her work with Laura off track:

Sharon: *But Laura, I just can't believe that God wants you to stay in a marriage where you're being degraded and abused.*

Laura: *I have to believe it, Sharon, because God said so, right here.*

As Sharon says of herself, mildly humorously but also humbly, "Now, having allowed myself to get into the advice-giving business, I go one big step further and set myself up as an expert on the Bible."

Sharon: *One of the things I've learned in my Bible studies at church is that a lot of things are attributed to Jesus in the New Testament he may not have ever said.*

Laura: *I've never heard of such a thing! If I allowed myself to think that for even a single moment, my faith would crumble.*

With a sigh of gratitude, Sharon tells her peers that she at least resisted the temptation to say to Laura what was racing through her mind at that moment:

Sharon: *Well, Laura, the faith you do have doesn't seem to be helping you much right now, does it?*

A little bit of knowledge about the Bible can be a dangerous thing. Solid Bible study inspires in us a greater enthusiasm for and appreciation of all that biblical faith can mean for us in every situation of our lives. However, it can also arouse in us such a strong desire to share with others what we have learned for ourselves that in shepherding situations we may momentarily lose sight of our primary responsibility. Our task as shepherds is to pay close attention to what our care receivers are saying to us rather than to what we can't wait to say to them.

Momentarily deflated by Laura's response to her "Jesus couldn't have said that" statement, Sharon tries to recover with another insight from her Bible class.

Sharon: *Okay, then why don't we look at the whole passage you quoted from and see what else is there?*

Laura: *If you think it'll help.*

Sharon: *I think it just might. What about our reading it out loud? You take one verse and I'll take the next, and so on. Okay?*

Laura: *It starts at verse 2, and it looks like it goes over to verse 9. (Laura and Sharon read from the King James translation.)*

And the Pharisees came to him, and asked him, Is it lawful for a man to put away his wife? tempting him. And he answered and said unto them, What did Moses command you? And they said, Moses suffered to write a bill of divorcement, and to put her away. And Jesus answered and said unto them, For the hardness of your heart he wrote you this precept. But from the beginning of the creation God made them male and female. For this cause shall a man leave his father and mother, and cleave to his wife; and they twain shall be one flesh: so then they are no more twain, but one flesh. What therefore God hath joined together, let not man put asunder.

Now Sharon is on to something. She is encouraging Laura to look at the context of a scriptural verse before concluding prematurely what the particular verse means. Once they finish reading the passage, Sharon needs to encourage Laura to share anything that she might think about it.

Sharon: *I'm glad we've started looking at everything Jesus said about divorce; it's gotten me thinking. But you first. What sorts of thoughts or feelings are you having?*

It would be too much to expect that Laura would suddenly see her situation in a different light as a result of the exercise she and her shepherd did together. It is more likely for Laura to react this way:

Laura: *To be honest, I can't see that it makes any difference. God's law is higher than Moses' law, and God is telling me not to divorce Rob.*

But whether this would have been her reaction, we will never know. For Sharon did not give her a chance to react. Instead, she did Laura's work for her.

Sharon: *To me, this is all about a dispute between Jews over how to interpret their laws in the first century. Do we have to take it as applying to us*

literally in the same way?
Laura: *Our pastor says that we can't pick and choose from the Bible ... we have to take all of it.*
Sharon: *If it's all or nothing, and this is what it says about divorce, I think I might have to take the nothing option.*
Laura: *Don't even think something like that. That's a sin against God!*

By this time Sharon finally is aware that pushing her views about how to read the Bible can only make things worse for her care receiver. She is of no more help than Laura's pastor was when he confirmed to her what her mother says:

Pastor: *Laura, divorce is not an option for a Christian woman. Jesus plainly taught that it is a sin, and if you pursue this course your soul will be in jeopardy.*

As if in the middle of a sentence, Sharon stopped talking, paused briefly, took a deep breath, and said:

Sharon: *Here I am, going on and on as if I really knew what I was talking about, and I haven't been here for you. You're scared to death about sinning against God and I'm prattling on about what I'm getting out of my Bible class.*
Laura: *(tearfully, but with a smile on her face) All is forgiven.*
Sharon: *Thank you—I really appreciate that. I only wish you could believe it for you, too.*

Though Sharon does not realize it at the moment, what she here says provides the opening she is looking for to help Laura find not only judgment but also grace in the Scriptures. The conversation continued.

Laura: *All I can see from what we read is that God will condemn me if I divorce Rob.*
Sharon: *It certainly does say that divorce is a very serious thing, and that it is a sin.*
Laura: *And sinners go to hell!*
Sharon: *Now I'm having a little trouble seeing that in what we read.*

Sharon is back on track! She is paying close attention to what is going on in Laura rather than in herself, and with Laura she is listening carefully to what the biblical text is and is not saying:

Laura: *Well, it may not be right at that exact point, but the Bible teaches us that the wages of sin is death.*
Sharon: *Do you read the Bible as saying that everywhere?*
Laura: *Yes! Well, maybe ... I guess not everywhere, but most places.*

Sharon: *In places where it doesn't say this, what does it say to you?*
Laura: *(after a long pause) The verses I'm thinking of now talk about God's love ... mercy ... (begins to cry)*
Sharon: *"There is now no condemnation ..." Laura, do you know where that verse is? I don't.*

Once Sharon sets aside her fascination with various theoretical questions preoccupying New Testament scholars—about which words alleged to be Jesus' are and are not his, and about whether or not standards for the first century apply equally in our own—she is able to lead Laura to hear in the Scriptures God's word of grace and forgiveness. That word comes to all of us just as we are, as sinners in need of redemption. God wants us to acknowledge our sins and to feel remorseful over them. Laura understands this much of the gospel message thoroughly. But God also reaches out to us, precisely in our sinful condition, with an invitation to accept his love for us in spite of our shortcomings and failures and to claim for ourselves the glorious freedom Jesus Christ has made possible for us, now and forever. Laura does not understand this part of the gospel message as well, and because she does not, she is drowning in the misery of a situation she believes can never change.

LEARNING FROM THE ILLUSTRATION

What can we learn from Sharon's work with Laura about our uses of the Scriptures with care receivers? We can learn what Sharon had to learn again on the spot: our care receivers' reading of the Scriptures, and not our own, is where we must begin. This is true no matter how different their reading may be from ours.

We can be put off by one care receiver's naive, almost childlike biblical literalism:

> If one man hadn't sinned six thousand years ago, the world wouldn't
> be in the shape it's in today.

And by another's frantic searching of biblical passages for some rule that can be applied unthinkingly to a present concern:

> Homosexuality is an abomination in the sight of God.

We can become impatient with still another's off-handed relegation of the Bible to an ancient history only:

> Look at what those first families were like—are we supposed to let
> them be our models?

In these instances, and in many others like them, neither our puzzlement, irritation, nor disdain is relevant. What is relevant is whether our care receivers see things in God's world more clearly through scriptural passages that are important to them. Telling them how we think they ought to apply a text would be like lending them our personal prescription glasses. The glasses are not likely to work for them, because their eyes are different from ours.

Does this mean that we can neither question nor challenge a care receiver's use of the Bible, that we have no right to suggest an alternative? Hardly. For example, we see that at two places in her shepherding, Sharon explicitly offers Laura another way to look at her situation in the light of the Scriptures that had become a stumbling block. First, Sharon attempts to bring Laura to acknowledge that God respects her as a person as much as he desires married people to stay married. Then Sharon invites Laura to explore some troubling words of Jesus by looking at the whole situation to which they were addressed. Sharon's efforts to get Laura to consider things from another angle of vision are like getting her to use distance rather than reading lenses. Laura is focusing on details at hand and missing a much bigger picture.

Though Sharon gets caught up for a time in promoting her way of looking at the Scriptures as the right way—looking at instead of through the lenses—she nevertheless grasped well one of the most highly respected principles of modern Bible study, the acknowledgment of context. Just as each individual verse in the Bible must be read in the context of the chapter and book in which it appears and the setting to which it was originally addressed, each passage of the Bible also points us to other passages that speak of the same things and sometimes from different standpoints. Most translations of the Bible bear witness to this fact by creating columns on each page of text that identify other passages of Scripture to which we ought to refer as we study the passage before us. For example, alongside the eight verses from Mark that Laura and Sharon read together, the King James Version lists no fewer than sixteen passages from other books in the Bible that are pertinent to the Markan one. In our celebration of the birth of our Lord, we typically do not rely on either Luke's or Matthew's version alone. We use both versions, freely mixed. And John's Gospel reminds us that we can feel the full force of the Incarnation without appealing to a birth and infancy narrative.

Thus far we learn two things from Sharon's shepherding of Laura about using the Scriptures with our care receivers. The first is that we need to pay more attention to the meaning our care receivers find in the texts than to what we get out of them on our personal faith journey. Second, we must respect the context in which each scriptural verse rests and the fact that complementary passages elsewhere in the Scriptures shed some light on any particular verse(s) with which we may be struggling. Important as these two considerations are, a third is more important still. We can get to it by taking up again the conversation between Sharon and Laura.

Earlier we paused in the conversation at Sharon's faltering reference to another scriptural text about condemnation:

> "There is now no condemnation." Laura, do you know where that verse is? I don't.

In one sense, it is a good thing that Sharon does not know exactly where to find what she is looking for. Her not knowing allows Laura to contribute more to the ensuing discussion than she might have otherwise, and it puts them on a more equal footing with respect to searching the Scriptures for God's word in the here and now. However, in spite of the fact that Sharon is not completely familiar with the terrain on which she ventures, she nevertheless is aware of something vital that her care receiver has yet to learn. Sharon gropes for the still larger context of the Bible's all-encompassing message, in the hope that Laura's fear of God's judgment can be tempered by her trust in God's mercy. Sharon's hope is well placed. Not surprisingly, Laura knows by heart the verse Sharon is searching for.

> There is therefore now no condemnation to them which are in Christ Jesus, who walk not after the flesh, but after the Spirit. For the law of the Spirit of life in Christ Jesus hath made me free from the law of sin and death. (Romans 8:1-2, KJV)

What Sharon knows but cannot express well is that the diverse messages we find in the Bible, some threatening to our core, must be seen in light of the one message of the Bible itself. That one message is a message about mercy and forgiveness. It is a message about the power of our almighty, supremely holy, and ever-loving God to bring and hold together everything in all creation in accordance with God's gracious, loving purpose and will:

> O give thanks unto the LORD; for he is good: for his mercy endureth forever. (Psalm 136:1, KJV)

> Therefore if any man be in Christ, he is a new creature: old things are passed away; behold, all things are become new. All things are of God, who hath reconciled us to himself by Jesus Christ, and hath given to us the ministry of reconciliation; to wit, God was in Christ, reconciling the world to himself, not imputing their trespasses unto them; and hath committed unto us the word of reconciliation. (1 Corinthians 5:17-19, KJV)

This one message serves as our lenses through which to see everything else—in the Bible, in ourselves, and in the world.

The conversation between Laura and Sharon continues.

Laura: *I do believe in a loving God, and that my Savior loves me too.*

Sharon: *Even if you divorce Rob?*

Laura: *I know it would be a sin.*

Sharon: *Would it be an unforgivable sin?*

Laura: *I know that Jesus would still love me.*

Sharon: *No matter what?*

Laura: *No matter what. It says so right in the Bible, doesn't it?*

Sharon: *Laura, between the two of us, you're by far the better Bible student. You've taught me a lot, and I'm very grateful to you. But yes, to me, too, it says it right in the Bible.*

Laura: *But Sharon, you're the one who's helping me see things more clearly.*

Sharon: *I think we're both seeing things better right now.*

THE SCRIPTURES AS LENSES: APPLICATION

This chapter began with Calvin's image of the holy Scriptures as a set of lenses through which we can see God's work and God's will in the world. Calvin's image becomes our point of reference for considering the uses and misuses of Scripture in shepherding relationships. As we follow one shepherd's work with her frightened and guilt-ridden care receiver, we discover three particularly helpful applications of the image of lenses. First, listening carefully and patiently to our care receivers' readings of the Scriptures is like acknowledging the importance of the lenses that are prescribed uniquely for them and respecting the Holy Spirit as the diagnostician and lens maker. By contrast, putting the emphasis on helping our care receivers to get a scriptural passage right, as we see it, is like forcing them to read the passage by means of our reading glasses, which may or may not fit their vision requirements.

Second, overreacting to a single verse, passage, or idea in the Scriptures is like using lenses appropriate for close-up work when we need lenses that help us to see more things across greater distances. Because the things of which the Scriptures speak always make their appearance in a larger field of view, they can be misperceived drastically when the context of a particular passage is lost sight of. Another way of putting this point is to say that prooftexting—citing one verse after another, out of context, in order to demonstrate what we were convinced about before we looked at any scriptural texts—is like purposely straining our eyes.

The third and final application of Calvin's comparison of the Scriptures with lenses has to do with the recognition that though there are many books in the Bible and that they sometimes differ considerably in theme and content, there is also a message of the Bible. There are many ways to express this message, because there are many passages from within the Scriptures that capture eloquently what God wants us to glean from them as a whole. Every shepherd will have favorite verses with which to express what the Bible is all about. Some of my own favorites are:

> And when we cried unto the LORD God of our fathers, the LORD heard our voice. (Deuteronomy 26:7, KJV)

> God so loved the world that he gave his only Son, that everyone who has faith in him may not perish but have eternal life. (John 3:16, REB)

> I am the Alpha and the Omega, the Beginning and the End. I will give water from the well of life to anybody who is thirsty. (Revelation 21:6, JB)

Looking at life situations by means of less than the one message of the Bible, whatever passage we may choose in the Bible to express it, is like trying to see what is in front of us with lenses that have cracks or mud all over their surfaces. By contrast, looking at those situations with a firm grasp of the Bible's message in its fullness is looking at them the way our God does—with an eye toward new possibilities, new life, new relationships, and a new world.

Most care receivers have their own ideas about what the Bible is all about. As the conversation between Laura and Sharon shows us, these ideas can have a profound effect on how a care receiver looks at his or her situation. Good shepherding encourages care receivers to bring these ideas into clear view, to test them by reference to the Bible's good news about what God has done in Jesus Christ, and to incorporate the perspective they gain from the exercise into a more obedient and abundant life, now and in all the years to come.

SOME QUESTIONS TO THINK ABOUT

1. Who are some of the people who helped you most to understand and appreciate the Bible? What do you consider to be their greatest contribution(s) to your making the Bible a resource for your growth in faith?
2. How well equipped do you feel yourself to be at present to help other persons get more out of the Bible for themselves?
3. What passage from the Bible most fully expresses for you what the message of the Bible as a whole is all about? Why does this particular passage hold the importance it does for you?

20. You Can Do It, and
You Don't Have to Do It Alone

THE BASIC PREMISE OF THIS BOOK IS THAT AS COMMITTED CHRISTIANS, ALL of us want to be of help to others in the name of Jesus Christ, but at times most of us harbor doubts about our abilities to provide the kind of help that we know others need. These doubts can be especially painful when we acknowledge that the ministry of caring for others is a task of the whole church and not just of the clergy. This chapter explores the major sources of such doubts, with an eye toward what we can do to overcome them.

WHO AM I, TO BE SOMEONE'S SHEPHERD?
Paradoxically, the major source of our doubts may be what is also the central concept of this book, the concept of the pastoral ministry of the laity. Though we pay great respect to this concept, we can still find it a difficult one to lay hold of. Why? Because its language seems to imply something else and because the church has honored more the something else than it has the fundamental principle. For many people, the term "pastoral ministry" means the caring ministry of the pastor. And if this is so, how can laypersons minister pastorally to others?

Such misunderstanding has pervaded pastoral practice almost from the beginning, to the extent that even today many are made to feel that only a pastor or a priest is authorized to care for the souls in congregations and that only a clergyperson's caring acts count as care. The wrongness of such a restrictive and oppressive view should be much clearer than it has been in the church. For the primary biblical meaning of pastoral has to do not with defining who the caregiver is (e.g., the pastor) as it does expressing the manner of care God expects from and for his people: care like a shepherd renders to his or her flock. When the concern is to point out the identity of the principal caregiver in relation to God's chosen people, the Bible turns our attention not to leaders of congregations but to God and Christ. In the words of a cherished gospel hymn: "Like a shepherd he leads us; much we need his tender care."

The convictions expressed in the previous paragraph have shaped my teaching and practice of pastoral care and counseling for many years. And yet, I must confess, they are convictions that I have had to struggle constantly to maintain. The major factor in the struggle has been my professional identity as a clergyman, theologian, and seminary professor. All three roles have been immensely satisfying in themselves, and in all three I believe I have been able to make at least a few modest contributions to others. In each, however, I have had to confront a major force that has divided clergy and laity almost from the beginning and that threatens the integrity and the future of the church in the present. Simply put, it is the pressure to place knowledge of faith's mysteries in the hands of a privileged few.

One way to get at my concern is by way of a liturgical expression familiar to many; "Christ has died; Christ is risen; Christ will come again." These words put powerfully before us the one, overarching, all-encompassing truth that has been, is, and likely ever shall be the foundation of our faith. It is the truth by which, in which, and for which we live as Christians in the world. But, as the liturgy reminds us, the formula expresses a mystery given to us for contemplation and trust rather than an assertion capable of being understood and explained on a rational level alone. We may and do say a lot about the formula, but its inner meaning finally rests deep in God's being and creative purposing. We trust that the affirmation expresses what is so for us, without knowing either that or how it is so. Acknowledging the necessity for trust in the absence of certainty has centered the faith of the church from biblical times to the present.

This crucial acknowledgment quickly gets forgotten in the heartfelt desire to communicate clearly to a desperate world what the Christian faith has to offer. But the more we talk about Jesus Christ and his saving work on our behalf, however sincere our intentions, the more we begin to sound knowledgeable, in possession of something an ignorant and doomed world will never be able to understand without our help. Then, the faith that God in Christ offers to all becomes perversely distorted by our imposing rigid limits on who shall be permitted to transmit it authoritatively to others. It is difficult to prevent the distortion. The foundation of faith is a great mystery that equalizes every Christian's position before it. But deep thinking about that mystery—including thinking about what the mystery implies for Christian action in the church and the world—is an important part of the Christian community's responsibility to be faithful to God's revelations in Christ. If we are to prevent the distortion that would disenfranchise laypeople from ministry, we must at all costs strive against entrusting the responsibility to think hard about faith only to a qualified few.

I am somewhat painfully aware at this stage of my ministry that, as I have attempted to fulfill my professional calling responsibly, I have taken far greater delight than I might have in being one of those qualified to say things about the great mysteries of faith on behalf of those who have had the right and the responsibility to speak for themselves. I am not alone in my elitism. Almost every well-trained theologian, pastor, and counselor with whom I have ever worked shares it. And we do so in spite of the fact that practically all of us also share the same conviction that ought to banish elitism forever. The conviction is that the church intended by God is composed of all Christians in ministry together, whose clergy occupy servant positions only. The actions that clergy take on behalf of others are to be taken on the basis of their own lively faith shared and reflected upon by other laypeople who also are the guardians and transmitters of the "faith once received by the saints." My temptations to elitism, along with those of my professional colleagues, are reinforced constantly by laypeople who are willing to leave these sorts of things to the professionals, so that they will not have to be responsible for translating their own faith into caring and effective action on behalf of others.

EVERY CHRISTIAN A SHEPHERD

What, then, do these considerations imply for the church's ministry of pastoral care? First, that God calls each of us, layperson and clergyperson, to trust in God's promises and deeds in Jesus Christ and to be part of a caring community of faith committed to sharing with others our response to those promises and deeds. Second, that God expects all of us in our various communities of worship and service to help each other grow in the knowledge of Christ's love experienced through the Holy Spirit, and together to live out ever more earnestly God's will for us and for all humankind. Third, that God equips us in every way to share his forgiving and transforming love whenever and wherever God presents opportunities to do so. And finally, that God rejoices with us when our own joy is made full by risking being a caring presence to others in his name.

In short, laypersons need not shy away from genuinely pastoral (i.e., shepherding) service out of fear of encroaching upon their pastor's or their priest's sacred duties. By referring to a clergyman or clergywoman as the shepherd of a flock, we honor that person's responsibility and capacity as the leader of a congregation. However, this in no way diminishes the shepherding ministry of that congregation. The final purpose of all shepherding, clergy and lay, is to help members of flocks to become better shepherds to others.

Ministering without Being Ministered To

It is easier to say all of this than it is to live it out in our ministry. We may know at a deep level that God will be with us in all of our prayerful efforts to be good shepherds, and still we may be besieged by one kind of self-doubt or another. For example, we might hold back from living our faith caringly for others from our not feeling adequately nurtured by the church, in spite of our personal dedication and service to it. We may believe that our spiritual deprivation might get in the way of anything that we might attempt to do with and for another person in need. And in part, we may be right. "We love because we have been loved first," wrote the author of the first Johannine letter. He saw clearly how difficult it can be to try to give to our neighbors in need a kind of love that we have not yet received ourselves. We might find that we lack energy and staying power for the task. Or we might let the other's positive responses to us become a principal source of our emotional gratification.

Nevertheless, it is possible to nurture others even though we may not have been adequately nurtured. The best evidence for believing so is the evidence of the shepherding experience. It is nothing short of remarkable how consistently shepherds speak to each other about their caregiving: "I'm getting so much more than I'm giving!" Should this surprise us? Hardly. For God is in the midst of our shepherding, blessing us and our care receivers at the same time. God's beloved Son taught us that in giving of ourselves, we will truly receive the blessings of life that our Father intends for us, that we will find life by losing it for the sake of others.

God's Answer to Burnout

Perhaps some of our self-doubts spring from another sort. If we seem to be indifferent to the plight of others, both in others' minds and in our own, it might be that in the past we have cared too much. It may be that our life history includes too many unsuccessful efforts to reach out, too many offerings of ourselves going unnoticed or unappreciated, and even being rejected.

Rebuffed too often, even the most well intentioned of us can become overwhelmed with disappointment, frustration, and a failure of resolve that is painful to confess and to overcome. Having fallen victim to empathy burnout, we may be unwilling to risk putting ourselves out for anyone else anytime soon.

To those of us who may suffer the frustration and disappointment of having our previous nurturing efforts go unnoticed or be rejected, our faith says: When God asks that we give of ourselves without thought of any earthly reward, it is to carry out God's purposes for the ones he asks us to care about. The satisfactions God wants us to experience from our shepherding will come, though, from a Spirit-filled sense of working with and pleasing God, whatever may be the response of another to our ministry. And just as God is with us in all that we attempt to do for another, he will give us the enthusiasm we need to fulfill our tasks.

I Can't Do It Myself

Another source of self-doubt is closely related to the previous one. One layperson I know expressed its essence simply and eloquently: "I knew I was in over my head, but I didn't know how to get out." Many of us who carry negative memories about our caregiving experiences acquired those memories because we were thrust into the middle of others' struggles and pain without adequate training for what was expected of us and without the ongoing support and nurture we deserved in order to accomplish our task. That pastoral care is the ministry of the laity is a fundamental and profoundly simple affirmation of our faith. Fulfilling its demands, however, is by no means easy. No one can do it without being called and equipped to do so. And no one can or should attempt to do it alone.

To those of us who have not as yet experienced success in offering care to others because we have not been trained and supported adequately in the task, our faith says: Though we have as yet to experience the church's best insights into shepherding for ourselves, the Christian community has known how to care well for its own, and for all of God's creatures, from the beginning. Both its wisdom and its support are available to us now.

What If My Faith Isn't Strong Enough?

Finally, some of us may hold back from caring for others because we are in doubt about the depth, integrity, wholeness, adequacy, or cogency of our personal faith. "How can I pray with someone else," a good friend said to me recently, "when I'm struggling so much with my own prayer life?" Or, as another shared, "I worry about having to tell another anything about God's grace, because I sometimes feel myself to be so unworthy in God's eyes." In my experience, the most deeply spiritual among us feel this concern most keenly. They know better than most that Christian caring for others must be more than (although no less than) merely an expression of one human being's concern to a fellow human being. They know that their actions toward another are to be offered in the name of Christ and that those actions witness to their personal faith and to the faith of the Christian community at all times and everywhere. Because they know this, they are rightly concerned that their own faith and understanding be up to the task.

To those of us who may harbor doubts about the adequacy of our personal faith, the faith we share together says: The best way to develop a strong and vital faith is by becoming a part of God's caring community now, encouraging one another in prayer, learning more together about the Scriptures, and supporting each other's striving to live as God in Christ lived for a suffering world. We can come into that kind of community confident that God will give us the faith we need. We do not have to build it by ourselves.

The most important thing that I have been trying to say in this book is that the nurturing ministry of the church does not rest in the hands of pastors and priests alone, distinctive as their contributions are and must be to that ministry. It rests with all Christians, together. As we set about pastoral work on his behalf, God will ask of all of us not that we do it perfectly but only that we do it prayerfully, together, learning from our mistakes and in our successes giving only God the glory. This book has sought to make the work easier, more enjoyable, and enriching to our growth in faith.

SOME QUESTIONS TO THINK ABOUT

1. God's gift of himself to you in Jesus Christ contains within it a call to discipleship that includes caring for others in Christ's name. At this stage in your life, do you feel ready to accept that call for yourself? Do you feel God's presence in your life, equipping you to fulfill it? What would help you most in becoming an effective shepherd to someone else?

2. What are your principal reservations about entering the shepherding ministry of your congregation? What would help you most in dealing with them?

3. Many people who give of themselves speak of their commitments as arising from the acknowledgment that it was time to give something back. Is this a time for you to give back? For what are you especially grateful in your life, for which you might give of yourself in return?

TRAINING MANUAL
A Program for Lay Shepherds

Section 1:
Equipping for Shepherding

The purpose of this manual is to apply *A Pastor in Every Pew* to the training of lay ministers of pastoral care in local congregations. These sections are designed to provide pastors and interested laypersons the material their congregations need to develop a program of lay training that can achieve high quality without placing heavy demands on church budgets and staff.

The kind of lay pastoral care with which we are concerned consists primarily of one-to-one shepherding offered in the name of Jesus Christ. For it to be effective, the shepherds need initial training. Further, they need the ongoing support of their fellow shepherds. Finally, they need the affirmation of a faith-filled congregation. Establishing an effective program of lay pastoral care requires addressing the third of these needs first.

Congregations well suited to support a ministry of lay shepherding are those served by pastors who believe strongly that Christian ministry is properly the work of all Christians. The pastors who share this belief make use of every opportunity to encourage their parishioners to minister to the congregation and the community. In these congregations are laypersons willing to consider a call to the ministry of caring for others and to commit sufficient time and energy to fulfill that call. Surrounding them is a larger cadre of church members who strengthen their pastor and lay shepherds with their sustained affirmation, referrals, and prayers.

If this description fits your congregation, then the lay shepherds whom the congregation enlists can invest themselves in ministry with the confidence that they are part of a truly caring Christian fellowship eager to be about God's work in the world. If this description does not fit your congregation, proceed cautiously about committing yourself to this form of service. To be most effective, lay shepherding must be, and must be perceived as, a representative ministry. It re-presents, that is, makes present

146

again, the aspirations and the commitment of the community of faith that sponsors it. If you as a lay shepherd cannot have a sense of connectedness with a vital and caring community of faith, no matter how caring a person you may be, your enthusiasm for shepherding others during difficult times will wane.

These sections are written for Christians in congregations caring enough to support them in a ministry of shepherding. The material primarily focuses on the first and second needs listed: the initial training and the ongoing peer support of the lay shepherds whom those congregations invite to serve. All of the sections presuppose that

- conversations have already taken place between a congregation's pastor and key lay leaders about establishing a program of lay shepherding;
- the congregation has been informed about these conversations and is enthusiastic about moving forward with a program;
- leaders are in place for the training and ongoing support of the congregation's lay shepherds;
- a procedure is in place for determining those members of the congregation who seem called to and gifted for the ministry of shepherding;
- a procedure is in place for getting people in need in contact with the lay shepherds who are qualified to help them; and
- time is devoted in worship services to calling the congregation's attention to the ministry of its lay shepherds, to commissioning lay shepherds at specific times of the year, to inviting church members to request a lay shepherd when they have need, and to praying for the ministry of the lay shepherds.

The first shepherding need is the need for initial training. Lay shepherds should be well trained, they should feel well trained, and they should approach their ministry to others with confidence as a result of that training. A word to pastors: you may feel that it is primarily your responsibility to train all your lay shepherds. If your time permits, your exercise of this responsibility can reap rich spiritual rewards for your congregations and your lay shepherds. For most of you, however, time does not permit your assuming the sole responsibility for all the training that you will

Training Manual

want your lay shepherds to receive. However, most congregations are blessed with highly competent laypersons who are more than willing to equip other church members for the ministry of shepherding. Ask for their help. You will not be shirking your own duty. In fact, the best training teams are composed of an involved pastor and capable laypeople working together with contagious enthusiasm.

The second shepherding need is the need for peer group support, following lay shepherds' initial training. Nothing is more important to the long-term future of a lay shepherding program than meeting this need. Many people get excited about the possibilities of lay pastoral care at the beginning. Few remain excited unless they experience the warmth, mutual caring, and challenge that comes when caring Christians share regularly the joys and concerns of their ministry. All lay shepherds should expect to participate actively in peer support groups for as long as they continue to work with care receivers.

With the sustained prayers and hopes of a caring community of believers, a well-planned training program, and a committed fellowship of caregivers, lay shepherding brings new life and liveliness to the nurturing ministry of congregations. May it be so for you and your congregation!

Section 2:
One More Time, into the Book!

The training outlined in these sections is based on the content of *A Pastor in Every Pew*. Some churches may choose to offer a short course on this book and go no further. The book's design permits use as a general introduction to caring from the perspective of our Christian faith. Though a discussion of its chapters in small groups will not by itself equip its participants to fulfill the responsibilities of lay ministers of pastoral care, it can provide significant help to people who want to express their caring more effectively in their families, on the job, and in all their relationships. It can also be the first step of a more intensive training program.

To offer a general-interest study, churches might consider organizing a twelve-hour Caring Christians course that devotes one hour to each of chapters 3 through 8, 10, 13, and 16 through 19. Sessions of two hours each, combined with one or two half-day retreats, would facilitate working through this material in four to six weeks. In a subsequent training course, attention can be given to chapters 9, 11, 12, 13, and 15, chapters not covered in the general-interest study.

As an aid to individuals who choose to read the book for their own purposes and to groups of people who elect to study the book, I have included at the end of each chapter Some Questions to Think About. Most of the questions are designed primarily to encourage self-reflection. Self-reflection is necessary to identifying issues and agendas in our lives that concern us. Although these issues are important to us, they can make it difficult to concentrate on what concerns our care receivers. By way of examples:

- Jan's horror stories of childhood neglect or abuse bring back painful memories of your growing-up, and you are uncertain whether to share some of them with her;
- Dan's graduation from West Point arouses in you a yearning to tell his father, Joe, how painful it was to you when you didn't get into the Naval

Academy, and you find yourself about to rain on Joe's parade;

- You throw things around after you get home from listening to Harriet's update on her messy divorce, and you realize how angry you still are at your ex-husband;
- Jim's toleration of his teenage son's drinking arouses in you a surprising amount of irritation that seems inconsistent with your commitment to moderation is the best policy;
- Nora's tears over the death of her husband bring you to the edge of sobbing in her presence, and you spend the rest of the session struggling to stay composed;
- Alice, with many needs of her own, courteously asks you how your week has been, and you realize ten minutes later that you have gone on and on about your mother's improving health, your daughter's good grades, and the joys you are experiencing playing tennis again;

and the list goes on!

Experiences like these are common in shepherding situations, and they are not signs of our ineptness. We are human. Our experiences, good and bad, sometimes invade even the most patient and capable focusing on another's needs. However, we are responsible for learning enough about ourselves to anticipate the kinds of situations in which we might listen less well because of what our care receiver may stir up in us. We also are responsible for letting our fellow shepherds help us with those aspects of our life and selfhood that might impede our being fully available to our care receivers.

There is another reason my questions are mostly invitations to self-reflection: our caregiving will become more effective when we begin to share at least some of what we learn about ourselves with trusted fellow shepherds. Such sharing can prevent us from unloading our stuff on our care receivers. We can unload it on our fellow ministers instead. And it can give us many rich experiences of being taken seriously, of being loved, and of being challenged by others who matter to us—the sorts of experiences that we want our care receivers to have with us.

At the close of the preface to *A Pastor in Every Pew,* I suggested that readers keep a journal to write out their answers to the questions. For most of us, writing our thoughts down enhances retention. Even more importantly, writing them down makes them easier to share with others. And so, I reiterate here the importance of taking the questions seriously enough to put answers to them in a personal journal.

Leaders of study groups will make their own decisions about how best to structure the discussions of the book's chapters. At the minimum, time should be given to summarizing the chapter contents, either by the leaders or by group members. Time should be provided for discussing group members' questions about the material. In my judgment, even more time should be given to group members' listening to each other's written self-reflections.

It is neither possible nor desirable to discuss every self-reflection question in a group setting. There is not enough time. Most groups will find it difficult to deal with more than one of the questions in the hour devoted to a particular chapter. Further, not everyone will be comfortable sharing all the things that may come out of their self-reflections. They should not be required to do so. As much sharing as possible should be encouraged, however, because the sharing can be the most important kind of practice that the participants will receive in what Christian shepherding is all about.

Christian shepherding is

- being available;
- encouraging and respecting trust;
- listening a lot and talking only a little;
- maintaining confidences;
- accepting another's disclosures without passing judgment;
- expressing God's grace, mercy, and love in ways appropriate to the care receiver's situation;
- resisting the temptation to fix things;
- helping the other to make his or her own decisions;
- praying with and for the other;
- searching the Scriptures for the word and the will of God for oneself and one's care receiver.

In the light of this list, groups studying *A Pastor in Every Pew* should make use of every opportunity to take stock of how caringly their members deal with one another's self-disclosures and of how supportive they are of one another's efforts to become more caring Christians in their everyday lives. At the beginning, group members should make a covenant with one another that everything they share about themselves will be held in confidence by the group.

Training Manual

Section 3:
Who Is Ready to Be a Shepherd?

This question is especially appropriate for those who discuss *A Pastor In Every Pew* together, who find it helpful in making everyday caring more effective, and who now want to become more involved in caring for people from an explicitly Christian perspective. Training to become a lay shepherd is one way toward such involvement. However, entering into such training should never be taken lightly or casually. It should represent a serious commitment of faith that follows an invitation by a congregation, and it should be expressed in a covenant. The following paragraphs offer suggestions to congregations for inviting their members to consider prayerfully the ministry of lay shepherding and for expressing their expectations in the form of a covenant for their lay shepherds.

Composing a statement of invitation provides an opportunity for a congregation to
- articulate clearly its understanding of the ministry of the laity;
- define what lay shepherds specifically do and not do;
- express the distinctively Christian components of all lay caregiving; and
- convey the distinctive mission of lay shepherding.

Here is one example of an invitation to consider the ministry of lay shepherding.

We Shepherd One Another
God calls all of us to care about and for others, in the name of our Lord Jesus Christ. One way to respond to God's call is by becoming a lay shepherd in our congregation. Lay shepherds receive special training to offer a ministry of Christian presence in times of need: illness, the death of a loved one, unexpected

crisis, divorce, job change, life transition, and the like. Lay shepherds are not counselors. They are supportive Christian friends who listen well, maintain confidences, encourage the sharing of feelings, and with their care receivers pray earnestly and search the Scriptures for God's guidance. Consider prayerfully God's call to care in your own life and whether it may include this important ministry of lay shepherding.

An invitation to church members to consider the ministry of lay shepherding should also make clear how and to whom those interested should make their response: e.g., to the pastor, the coordinator of lay training, or the program's chairperson. Further conversations with the designated person(s) can provide potential lay shepherds the essential information about the congregation's expectations of them and the training they will receive. These conversations can also serve an initial screening purpose, as they elicit pertinent information about potential caregivers and their reasons for wanting to become shepherds. Some congregations may issue its invitation to consider lay shepherding to one person at a time. Other congregations may address the whole membership at once, through announcements in the worship services, church bulletins, and the like.

Those who respond positively to the invitation to lay shepherding should be prepared to enter into a covenant before God and with their congregation, trainers, and peers. (If they have not read this book, they should be asked to do so before they go further.) The basic form of the covenant is a mutual pledge to offer the best that is in us, by God's grace, in order that God and not we may be glorified through the shepherding that we will offer in the name of Jesus Christ. Here is one example of a covenant statement that lay shepherds should be asked to sign at the beginning of their training.

A Shepherd's Covenant
With gratitude for God's all-surpassing love in Jesus Christ, and for God's loving presence in my life, I accept my congre-

gation's invitation to the ministry of shepherding in his name.

With God's help, I will seek diligently to become an effective caregiver to others, while recognizing and celebrating that healing, comfort, guidance and strength come finally from God.

I will faithfully participate in the training and growth opportunities offered me for as long as I remain a lay shepherd in this congregation.

In a spirit of love, I will remain open to the encouragement and the help that my fellow shepherds offer me, and I will support their every effort to serve God faithfully in their own ministry to others.

I will pray constantly for God's guidance in my care receiver's life and in my own.

The examples given are intended to be that and no more. Each congregation will have its own concerns to heed as the leaders of its lay shepherding program work out the kind of invitation and covenant statements that best suit their situation. What I want most to emphasize is the necessity of both kinds of statements to a high-quality program; however, each congregation may choose to formulate them for its purposes. They are so important that they deserve periodic review, and when necessary, revision.

Section 4:
Exercises to Get Started

These paragraphs provide an opportunity to practice and discuss the beginning of a shepherding relationship. Review chapter 9 of *A Pastor in Every Pew* before you do these exercises.

Lay shepherds' care receivers come to them by referral. The referrals may be from the pastor, from other church staff members, or from a leader of the congregation's lay shepherding program. On rare occasions a member of the congregation may approach you directly for help. Even though you are trained and may be the person for the task, you should not commit to being his or her caregiver without securing the approval of the person(s) in charge of overseeing all the referrals for your program.

At least one member of the program's leadership team should be responsible for maintaining (in strictest confidence) accurate records of all lay shepherding relationships, past and present. This will not be possible unless each lay shepherd receives word to proceed from the pastor or the referrals administrator.

Let us assume that a referral to you is in process. The following two cases presume that in the ministry of lay shepherding, women work with women and men with men. In this light, pick the situation that is appropriate for you.

Your pastor has called and has asked you to consider becoming a lay shepherd to (Joan Elliott)/(Bill Thompson). He has relayed the following information about your potential care receiver:

- Mrs. Elliott's husband died suddenly of a heart attack while they were on vacation in Hawaii. The pastor conducted the funeral in the church three weeks ago and has had two visits with Mrs. Elliott since then. Mrs. Elliott welcomes his offer of a lay shepherd.

- Mr. Thompson, long divorced, struggles with loneliness and declining health. Neither of his two grown children has shown an interest in maintaining a relationship, even for the sake of the grandchildren. Mr. Thompson seems willing to talk with someone, but he has some doubts about whether it will do any good.

You accept your pastor's invitation to be a caregiver to (Joan) (Bill), whom you do not know personally. Accordingly, your first task is to place a call to (her)/(him) to set a time and place for a face-to-face conversation.

An exercise for you: Write down in a few brief sentences what you would say to Joan or Bill when she or he answers the phone. Be prepared to share what you have written with other members of your training group.

An exercise for the group: Listen carefully for, and comment on, the following in others' opening statements:

1. The communication of empathy and a desire to be of help;
2. The expression of a genuine interest in meeting face to face, without pressuring the potential care receiver;
3. Careful listening, while encouraging the care receiver to save for the face-to-face meeting the details of his or her needs.
4. Keeping things brief and oriented to the main point of setting up the first meeting.

Now let us assume that you have set up your first conversation and are sitting with your care receiver, about to begin.

An exercise for you: In a few brief sentences write what you would say to get the conversation going and what you imagine your care receiver might say in response. Be prepared to share what you have written with other members of the training group.

An exercise for the group: Listen carefully for, and comment on, the following in other group members' statements:

1. The constructive uses of pleasantries to establish rapport;
2. The ease with which the lay shepherd moves from pleasantries to the business at hand;

3. The communication of positive interest in the care receiver's situation and a desire to understand it more fully;

4. The comfort level of the lay shepherd.

A final exercise for the group: In pairs, using the situations of Joan and Bill, role play an initial telephone call and then the initial five minutes of the first face-to-face meeting. Each shepherd should have the opportunity to play both the care receiver and the caregiver roles. Each shepherd should also have the opportunity to share with the group whatever he or she feels about readiness for getting a shepherding relationship started well.

Section 5:
What Do You Say after You've Said "I'm Here to Help"?

Practice, practice, practice! No matter what we want to do well, there is no substitute for practice. We practice baking cakes, swinging a golf club, playing the piano, or painting in watercolors. We practice on old car parts before we try to fix new cars. We try out our Spanish on tolerant friends before going abroad on our own. And if we are to become effective caregivers, we will have to practice that, too.

It is one thing to mix the ingredients of a cake, to hit at a golf ball, to crunch piano keys, to splash paint on a canvas, to put pressure on an old car's drive shaft, or to try to say "rest room" in Spanish. When we make mistakes doing these kinds of things, there usually is no harm done, except to our egos. But practicing our caregiving skills means trying them out on another person. If we don't do it right the first time, couldn't we do real harm? Yes, we could, and this is why we must practice before we shepherd someone in need. But how can we do this?

One of the best ways is through role play: playing the roles of a care receiver and of a shepherd, in front of people who are striving to become better caregivers themselves. In this kind of setting, we can be freed from our appropriate concern not to make things worse for someone while we are learning to make things better. The mistakes we make—and we will make them—will help us to learn how to minister more effectively without damaging anyone in the process. The support we receive from our peers in training will help us to develop needed confidence. Role playing and the feedback we get from it reassure us that we can be helpful and that by God's grace we will be helpful.

Your first assignment: Write out a brief description of a potential care receiver who needs the kind of ministry that a lay shepherd can provide. It is better to create a fictional person rather than to describe someone you know or may have known. Using your imagination will eliminate the possibility of breaking confidences or exposing someone's real distresses needlessly. Describe what this fictional care receiver is struggling with and the factors that have contributed to his or her problem(s). Now, get into the proper frame of mind to be that person, in a simulated shepherding session with a member of your group.

Group exercise: This exercise is done in groups of three. Eventually each member of the triad will take turns playing three roles, in the sequence mutually agreed upon: caregiver, care receiver, and observer. When you play the role of care receiver, use the fictionalized case that you created in the assignment above. Plan on a conversation with the person playing the role of caregiver that will last between twenty and twenty-five minutes. During the role play, the observer takes notes, mentally or on paper, but makes no comments until the end. Then the observer offers feedback on how he or she feels the conversation went, using the Observer's Checklist provided below. After the observer makes his or her comments, members of the triad should discuss their mutual reactions to the role play and to what the observer has said. Any questions that emerge from this discussion should be brought to the whole training group before members of the small groups change roles and proceed to round 2 and round 3.

Each of these three role plays will take from forty-five minutes to an hour to complete. The first time a training group does the exercise, it is better to complete all three rounds one after the other than it is to space them out across more than one session. Therefore, this part of lay shepherds' training ought to be scheduled at a time that will permit a meeting of at least three hours. A retreat format works best, because it allows members to relax together between each of the role plays, along with times for singing, devotions, and meals. Later, peer support groups of commissioned lay shepherds can use this exercise to sharpen skills, scheduling only one role play at any particular meeting.

In this exercise, the role of the observer is especially important. Two primary goals should influence how the observer makes his or her comments: identifying clearly what the caregiver has done well and offering whatever suggestions may be appropriate to help the caregiver do even better the next time around. By concentrating on these two goals, the observer sets a positive tone for the group's exploration of each role play.

The Observer's Checklist should be the basis for the observer's initial comments and group members' discussions of how well any particular role play did or did not go. The checklist is based on the characterization of what Christian shepherding is about, offered in section 1, and on the discussion of the basic conditions for all caring relationships, discussed in chapters 4 through 8 of *A Pastor in Every Pew*.

Observer's Checklist

1. Establishing Trust
- Did the shepherd seem at ease with the care receiver?
- Did the shepherd's demeanor seem genuine?
- How did the shepherd communicate his or her interest in what the care receiver was saying?

2. Listening
- Did the care receiver do most of the talking?
- How did the shepherd show understanding of and compassion for what the care receiver was feeling?

3. Accepting without Judging
- Did the shepherd seem respectful of the care receiver's feelings and actions or inaction?
- Did the shepherd show any signs of agitation, disagreement, or disapproval in his or her responses?
- How did the shepherd affirm and encourage the care receiver's decision-making abilities and responsibility?

4. Expressing God's Love
- How did the shepherd express God's presence and grace in the care receiver's life?
- How did the shepherd communicate God's love for the care receiver?

5. Praying
- Did the shepherd ask the care receiver if he or she wanted prayer?

Training Manual

- Did the shepherd invite, without pressuring, the care receiver to partic-ipate in praying together?
- How comfortable was the shepherd with prayer in this situation?

6. *Reading the Bible*

- In what ways did the shepherd either introduce or affirm the impor-tance of seeking God's will by reading from the Bible?
- How comfortable did the shepherd seem to be with talking about the Bible in this situation?

The fifteen questions that make up this checklist for observers are not intended to be exclusive or exhaustive. Observers and group members should feel free to bring up other matters for discussion as a particular role play may make appropriate. In most instances, however, they should provide your group a broad selection of questions that are likely to be worth pursuing. Since there will not be time, after a particular role play, to explore all fifteen questions, much less all the ones that group members may want to add, the key to a good discussion will be choosing the right questions for the material the role play presents.

Section 7 provides descriptions of some fairly typical care receivers' situations. The cases can be used in place of the fictional descriptions called for in the assignment above, and they can be used for other role-playing exercises in the context of follow-up training and support.

Section 6:
An Outline of Training Sessions

The outline to follow presupposes that participants have completed the twelve-hour course, Caring Christians, suggested previously. The training sessions include attention to chapters 9, 11, 12, 13, and 15, chapters not discussed in the general study of *A Pastor in Every Pew*. Training exercises used are those described in other sections. The training course outlined requires twelve hours, and it can be completed in four to six weeks.

Training Session 1   *2 hours*
Preparation: Read chapters 11 and 9

Devotional	10 minutes
Introductions: the course and its participants' goals	20 minutes
Topic 1: Confidentiality	30 minutes

Focuses on chapter 11 and follows the format of the congregation's small-group study and discussion of the book.

Break	5 minutes
Exercises 1, 2, and 3: Practicing Getting Started	50 minutes

Group members complete the exercises described in section 4. This part of the training is based on chapter 9.

Closing Prayers	5 minutes

Training Session 2   *2 hours*
Preparation: Read chapters 13 and 15

Devotional	10 minutes
Topic 2: Self-Disclosure	45 minutes

Focuses on chapter 13 and follows the format of the congregation's small-group study and discussion of the book.

Break	10 minutes
Topic 3: Assigning Tasks	45 minutes

Focuses on chapter 15 and follows the format of the congregation's small-group study and discussion of the book.

Closing Prayers	10 minutes

Training Session 3, retreat format   *6 hours*

This session is based upon the three role plays (exercises 4, 5, and 6) outlined in section 5, and it requires more time than any of the other training sessions. It provides an excellent context for dealing as well with chapter 12 of *A Pastor in Every Pew*. Most groups will find that a retreat setting is desirable for this part of the training and has the additional advantages that all well-planned retreats do: space, relaxation, group building, spiritual renewal. A six-hour format, from 9 until 3 on a Saturday, for instance, provides time for a morning devotional, an hour each for three role plays and discussion, lunch together, an hour's discussion of chapter 12 on mirroring, some time to deal with other questions that may have arisen in the role plays, and a closing eucharistic worship service.

Final Training Session   *2 hours*

Devotional   10 minutes

Exercises 7, 8, and 9   75 minutes
Group members role play three of the cases in section 7.

Preparation for Commissioning   30 minutes
This is a time for dealing with any remaining questions group members may have about what their commitment to the church will be as a lay shepherd (e.g., what the support groups will be like; how long they will be expected to serve; the kinds of care receivers they do and do not feel prepared to shepherd; details of the commissioning service and any accompanying celebration.

Closing Prayers   5 minutes

Using A Pastor in Every Pew in the ways outlined in these sections yields twenty-four hours of training for lay shepherds in Christian congregations. However, these twenty-four hours cover only the basics of caregiving from a Christian perspective. The peer support groups, to be described shortly, are essential to providing the next steps in equipping the saints for this unique ministry. If congregations ask for a one- to three-year commitment to the program, they will be able to provide their lay shepherds the ongoing support and accountability that these groups ensure.

Section 7:
Some Typical Shepherding Cases for Role Playing and Discussion

To this point we have described shepherding relationships that begin with a referral, are primarily one to one, and proceed from a mutual agreement to deal with one range of issues for as long as the care receiver feels the need. In the light of these considerations, I offer six cases as further resources for role play, reflection, and discussion.

Case 1. Harriett is a divorced, working mother of three. Her aging mother has lived with her for the past five years and now is in seriously declining health. Two of Harriett's children have difficulties at school. It has been two years since Harriett received her last pay raise, and she is beginning to have difficulty making ends meet. She feels overwhelmed and does not know where to turn for help.

Case 2. Kennie, who often bags your groceries at your favorite store, is standing near the cart return as you wheel your shopping cart to your car. He is puffing hard on a cigarette, and you notice several cigarette butts scattered around his feet. You are surprised and disappointed, because Kennie has told you these past six months about his attempts to give up smoking. You leave your grocery cart by the front entrance, frozen foods notwithstanding, and go over to him. You learn that his younger brother has been killed in a knife fight and that because no one in the family had money for his funeral, his brother was buried "in a field with lots of other no-accounts." Kennie is so grief-stricken that he can hardly talk.

Case 3. Roberta and Don are at their wits' end trying to cope with the problems of their oldest son, who by his sixteenth year has been arrested for shoplifting and suffers from a drug problem. Recently he was expelled from school. Don and Roberta are angry with their son but guilt-ridden over how they may have failed to be the kind of parents he needed earlier in his life. They fear what will happen to the boy if he does not turn his life around.

Case 4. Jean has been recovering from surgery to remove a malignant tumor in her breast. Though her primary physician seems pleased with how well she is doing, Jean expresses a great deal of anger toward God for "letting this happen." Her husband is irritated with her for not setting a good example by being stronger in her faith. Jean does not know how to deal with him. Her young children have confessed to one set of grandparents their terror that their mother is going to die. She does not know what to say to her children in response.

Case 5. Mildred, your eighty-five-year-old neighbor, has not sat on her front porch for two or three days, and you are concerned. Though her lights are on in the evening, she does not answer her telephone. You decide to check things out. Mildred responds quickly to your knock on her front door, invites you to come in and sit down, and then remains quiet for an uncomfortable interval of time. She finally begins to tell you that two of her dearest friends died in hospitals the previous week, and she is more worried than ever about what will become of her.

Case 6. Bill has been passed over for a promotion for the second time in two years and hears rumors that his company may soon be sold. He is a thirty-year employee who previously took it for granted that the company would take care of him and that he would advance still further before his retirement, some eight years off. Bill has no idea what he could do if he were to lose his job. He struggles with feelings of anger and fear that he is not sure he can handle.

One of the things that lay shepherds often discover, the more they get to be known as shepherds in the congregation, is that they will have many opportunities to provide shepherding without entering into a long-term shepherding relationship. These additional opportunities make a cadre of lay shepherds even more valuable to a congregation. Here are a few examples of how episodic your work as a lay shepherd might be:

- You spend a full day in and near a hospital waiting room, visiting with a number of family members who receive periodic progress reports on a long surgical procedure for a grandparent;
- The pastor telephones you at 3 A.M. to accompany him to the home of

a young woman, living alone, who has just been told of the death of her only remaining relative;

• While you are mowing your lawn on a hot summer morning, you notice your next-door neighbor sitting on his porch, sobbing;

• The president of your Sunday school class tells you that George Smith, a cherished member of the class, has been hospitalized for exhaustion, and George wants you to be the one to inform three family members who live out of state;

• The chair of your church's evangelism committee asks if you will contact a long inactive member to encourage him to return;

• One of your most valued employees comes into your office, distraught that his son is truant from school again and that no one can find him.

In all likelihood, few if any of these situations would lead to a formal, one-to-one shepherding relationship. Instead, most call for immediate attention on a one-time basis. Even so, the people in these situations deserve the best of which a shepherd is capable. A single conversation measured in minutes can call forth caregiving skills every bit as wide-ranging as many conversations with the same care receiver across many weeks and months. Capably trained shepherds should be prepared to respond to both kinds of need.

The cases and examples offered are intended only as additional resources to training groups whose members should be encouraged to supply material for role playing and discussion. When shepherds do present material from their imagination and experience, those responsible for a congregation's training program have at their disposal yet another way to increase the number of useful cases for training purposes. They can collect those produced by one generation of trainees and make them available to the next.

Training Manual

Section 8:
Shepherding the Shepherds

Throughout *A Pastor in Every Pew* I underscored that lay shepherds commit themselves to meet regularly for mutual support and sharing. This commitment is as fundamental to our integrity and effectiveness as is the commitment to put the needs of our care receivers first. The point is simple and basic: Participation in an ongoing support group of fellow caregivers is indispensable to faithful and effective shepherding.

Such a group serves two primary needs. The first is expressed accurately by the group's name: support. We need and deserve support for ourselves from people who know what we are going through. We need caring friends with whom we can share our frustrations, uncertainties, hopes, and prayers. In shepherding situations, not any friend will do. We need people around us who understand fully the ramifications of respecting and maintaining confidences. Remember: we can't do it alone, and we aren't alone.

The second need that a shepherding group serves is the need for accountability. This need is manifest on two levels: the sponsoring congregation and the shepherds. As members of congregations, we need and deserve assurance that all of our ministers, clergy and lay, are qualified to perform the tasks to which they are called, that our ministers' work is reviewed in a timely and competent manner, and that our ministers remain open to encouragement and to constructive criticism. As shepherds, we need and deserve assurance that our service is helpful and appreciated, that we are growing in grace and in the knowledge and love of Christ, and that the Holy Spirit is at work in what we do for our care receivers. Peer support groups provide an environment of grace in which we shepherds can make ourselves accountable to one another, in love, on both these levels of need.

The following paragraphs offer guidelines for establishing and maintaining support groups for lay shepherds. We begin with two reminders.

The first is that we enter into a covenant at the beginning of training to participate regularly in a peer support group for as long as we remain a lay shepherd in the congregation. Second, overall supervision of a congregation's lay shepherding program must be the responsibility of the pastor. With these considerations clear all around, those responsible to the pastor for equipping a congregation's lay shepherds can proceed to determine the leadership of the peer group(s).

Though pastors may devoutly wish to be peer group leaders, in most cases their other responsibilities to the congregation will make it next to impossible for them to do so. However, they can play a vital role by sharing the responsibility for training others to lead the ongoing peer groups. In many congregations, lay shepherds possess the capability and the desire to share leadership of the peer groups. In such situations, they might serve on a rotating basis. But one person must be designated as peer group(s) coordinator, and that person must bear the responsibility, through the pastor, of assuring the congregation that its lay shepherds function responsibly and grow spiritually in the process.

Three generally useful rules serve for planning peer support group meetings. The first is that meeting time should be distributed roughly evenly between giving group members support and asking them to be accountable to each other for their ministry. It will not be possible to follow this formula at every meeting. Care receivers' needs must take priority over the group's needs. But there will be times when the members' care receivers are doing well and the group can give more attention to what is going on in each other's lives. The overall balance of support and accountability is important, more than how that balance may be achieved in any particular session.

The second rule is that peer interaction goes best in groups of between five and eight. Small congregations with fewer than five lay shepherds might consider merging their training and peer group processes with those of one or more other small congregations. If there are more than eight lay shepherds in one congregation or cluster of congregations, another peer group should be created as soon as it is feasible to do so.

Training Manual

Where there are multiple peer groups, it is a good idea to rotate members periodically. The more of our peers we can hear from about our shepherding, the more effective our shepherding is likely to become.

The third rule is that as lay shepherds we will have sufficient material to share with our peers if we bring that material after no more than three sessions with a care receiver. Care receivers in crisis may make it imperative for us to report more frequently to the peer group. Shepherds who try to present material covering more than three sessions with their care receivers usually feel frustrated over not having enough time to talk about everything that they need to discuss.

With these three rules in mind, we can begin to make decisions about the frequency, duration, and agenda of our peer group meetings. With regard to the frequency of meetings, every two weeks across the year, with time off for major holidays and with recognition of necessary absences and vacation schedules, will prove to be about right for most programs. With regard to the duration of each meeting, groups of five or six likely will need around ninety minutes to accomplish everything that a good peer group meeting should accomplish, and groups of seven or eight will need at least two hours.

What happens in a peer group meeting? Here is one possible agenda.

Gathering/Announcements/Devotional   10-15 minutes

Nurturing the Shepherds   25-40 minutes
You are invited but never required to share a personal joy or concern and/or a personal prayer request, and members of the group respond as appropriate. Your sharing should be brief, to ensure that all who need the group's nurture can receive it. It is not likely that every member will share at every meeting.

Stretch Break   5 minutes

Reviewing the Caregiving   50-90 minutes

After the first caregiving session and after each set of three sessions following, you report to the group on your work, keeping the identity of your care receiver strictly confidential. Each report should include at least the following:

1. A brief description of the care receiver's situation, how well the care receiver seems to be coping with the situation, and what you think may be the care receiver's greatest need at present.

2. A statement, in a sentence or two, of what you and your care receiver have agreed to work on together and the circumstances under which you will be working (e.g., at the care receiver's home, in the hospital).

3. Some thoughts about how you see God working in this situation. What do you believe may be the most appropriate things for you and the group to bring to God in prayer for your care receiver?

4. Focusing your principal concerns as you begin or continue ministry with your care receiver. What would you like from the support group by way of help?

In a typical support group meeting, the group will discuss two reports. How many, however, will depend on the members' caregiving schedules. Some members will have completed three sessions with their care receivers and will be ready to report as a matter of course. One member may have just begun a new shepherding relationship and will need to report on the first session. Another may have finished with one care receiver and is awaiting another assignment, so has no report. Finally, priority must always be given a shepherd whose care receiver is in a major crisis. Sometimes this will mean that the time given to nurturing one another will have to be shortened. Or it may mean that another shepherd's report is postponed until the next meeting.

Closing Prayer Circle   5 minutes

This aspect of a lay shepherding program is vital to its success and longevity. Careful recruitment and high-quality training can put in place a ministry of lay pastoral care about which there will be high expectation and contagious enthusiasm—at the beginning. But the nurture and spiritual growth that hard-working shepherds can experience keeps the expectations high and the enthusiasm contagious.

Well-planned support group meetings will maintain morale and energy among a congregation's lay shepherds. Also of help are special events such as commissioning lunches or dinners, social gatherings around the holidays, and retreats. Rounding out congregations' ministry to their shepherds should be a solid program of continuing education: guest speakers, invitations to attend seminars and workshops elsewhere, and study opportunities as they arise. Shepherding our shepherds well will make their shepherding more effective, enriching, and exciting.

Training Manual

Section 9:
The Ministry of Referral

We can't do it all, but we don't have to. In every congregation and community, other capable helpers are available, once we make the effort to learn who they are and to seek them out.

Sometimes it is a matter of necessity to call out for additional help: e.g., when a care receiver struggles with an addiction, becomes suicidal, threatens violence, seems depressed out of proportion to losses suffered, experiences episodes of being out of touch with reality, or loses everything in a fire. Other times, it is more a matter of enhancing a care receiver's coping capacities: e.g., when a care receiver cannot drive anymore, needs help with a resume, feels overwhelmed with a child's difficulties in school, struggles with nursing home placement for an aging parent, has unresolved faith questions, or craves a deeper spiritual life. When our care receivers either need or can profit from additional help, it is our responsibility as their shepherds to help them get it.

How do we do this? First we become knowledgeable about the resources that are available in the congregation and community. Pastors can be primary sources of this kind of information. In addition, many churches have staff members or laypersons specifically charged to gather pertinent information about caregiving resources and to make that information available when there is need for it. Most social workers on hospital staffs and in community agencies are up to date in this area. And police departments can provide all kinds of guidance on where we can get help for people. Information about who can help is readily available. Our first task is to acquaint ourselves with it.

Our second task is to practice, in the presence of our peers, the delicate art of introducing to our care receivers the idea of securing the additional help that we believe they should have. Several things make this task a delicate one.

- Our care receivers may worry that if they need additional help, their condition is even worse than they have thought;
- They may receive our suggestion courteously and then promptly fail to follow up on it;
- They may think that we are handing them off to someone else because we do not want to be their shepherds anymore;
- They may reject our efforts to refer them and insist that we can provide all the care they need;
- They may accept our referral and prematurely terminate their shepherding relationship with us.

Referral is harder than it looks. The first principle that we must uphold as shepherds is to be honest. If we strongly believe that seeking additional help is desirable, we need to say so. If our care receiver disagrees, we must respect his or her point of view, but we must encourage a full exploration of it. If we strongly believe that seeking additional help is necessary, then, with the pastor's help, we must insist on securing it.

The second principle is to reaffirm presence. The process of referral in shepherding relationships is a process of seeking additional help. It is not a process of substituting something else for the shepherding relationship. Once our care receivers feel sufficiently reassured that we intend to continue being their shepherds for as long as it takes, then they are likely to feel more comfortable accepting the additional help that we make available to them.

Next to continuing in prayer with and for our care receivers, effecting a referral may be the most important thing that we can do for them. Doing it well also means that we do something important for ourselves. We remind ourselves anew that we are never alone in our ministry. God is with us. And so is a large host of caring people seeking to serve God faithfully in all that they do.

Group exercise: Each shepherd should have the opportunity to role play making a referral. Following the pattern of previous role plays, this exercise should be completed in small groups of three, with each member alternately playing the role of caregiver, care receiver, and observer.

The following cases should provide sufficient material for the exercise.

1. Anna is sixty years old, recently widowed, and has lived a sheltered existence with a husband who strongly affirmed his role as provider and his responsibility to see to it that she never had to worry about everyday details. She has never paid a bill, never taken a car for repairs, never dealt with a repair person. Overwhelmed with financial decisions that must be made soon, Anna is adamant that it would be disloyal to her husband's memory not to take full responsibility for these things herself. You believe that it would be in her best interest to hire a financial advisor.

2. George must undergo a risky surgical procedure soon and is angry with God for inflicting suffering not only on him but also on several members of his family over the years. As George shares some of the details, you become increasingly uncertain about what to say to him. You are clear that George needs to talk about some of these feelings with someone more spiritually gifted than you feel yourself to be.

3. Stella is beside herself with worry over her fourteen-year-old son, who has been expelled from school after officials discovered drugs in his locker. The expulsion is the latest in a series of crises dating back over two years. Her husband has a high-paying job that takes him out of the country for weeks at a time. He constantly berates Stella for not straightening things out at home, and Stella thinks that he is right. The couple has yet to seek out any professional help either for themselves or for their son.

4. Theresa, a thirty-eight-year-old mother of three teenage children, has been in and out of treatment for more than three years following surgery for breast cancer. Radiation and chemotherapy have not prevented other tumors, and Theresa has become increasingly despondent about her future. Her husband has had to assume more and more responsibilities at home, and Theresa speaks of being "worthless to everyone." She assures you that she has no thoughts of suicide, but you are deeply concerned about how depressed she is. You believe that medication or therapy for the depression may be called for.

Training Manual

5. Al has just been told that the division of his company, in which he has been employed for twenty years, will be phased out over the next three months. The severance package Al will receive is, in his words, "useless," and he feels frightened about how he will be able to provide for his family at a time of high need. He and his wife have two children in college and a parent with Alzheimer's disease. Al seems immobilized with anxiety. You know that he needs help, and you are especially concerned about his lack of motivation to seek it.

6. Brenda's husband of four years has just told her that he has hired a lawyer for the purpose of getting a divorce. "You'll need a good one yourself," he said, and Brenda is in shock. From what you know about Brenda's husband, you do not believe that he is likely to show any concern for her future well being, and you are worried about what might happen if Brenda does not get good legal advice soon. Part of Brenda's reluctance to seek it is her conviction that hiring a lawyer means giving up on the marriage.

Training Manual

Section 10:
Wounded Healers and Stricken Shepherds

In this final section we take up a difficult but crucial issue for the integrity of lay shepherding programs: our responsibility as members of Christian congregations for determining who is and is not suitable to become a shepherd to someone else. We cannot avoid this responsibility. All Christians are called to care for others to the extent of their abilities. But not all Christians are called to be others' shepherds.

A major theme of *A Pastor in Every Pew* is that Christian shepherds are not counselors. We are Christian friends, trained especially to listen, to honor feelings, to be nonjudgmental, to affirm strengths, to encourage openness to God's Word in the Bible, and to pray, all in the name of Jesus Christ. We share our care receivers' struggles to live more faithfully in response to what God has done for us in Christ, acknowledging our sins and shortcomings with hearts "unfeignedly thankful" for God's boundless love, mercy, and grace. In gratitude, we gladly share Christ's love in our commitment to care, and we anticipate that glorious day when we will truly find our greatest joy in putting others' needs above our own.

In all of this, we remain finite, imperfect, even wounded servants whose ministry must depend upon the Holy Spirit for its fulfillment. We cannot heal. We cannot cure. We cannot make all things new. But God can, even though he must work through our self-doubts, weakness of heart, impatience, impulses to fix, grandiose fantasies, and self-centeredness. Therefore, we do not have to do our work perfectly for our care receivers to experience God's healing and empowering. Further, we do not have to be perfect for them to experience the peace of God in our presence. At best, we can only be who we are: sinners who need God's grace but are striving nevertheless to let Christ dwell in our hearts more fully.

The fact that we are finite, imperfect, and wounded people does not disqualify us for the ministry of shepherding. If it did, God would have no shepherds on earth to do his work. But just as it does not disqualify us from serving our Lord, it does not qualify every one of us. Some people's limitations and woundedness will seriously impede their giving of themselves genuinely for others. Their own problems absorb so much of their energy that little is left over for anyone else. It is an awesome thing for our congregations to entrust someone's well being to one of our shepherds. Because it is such a profound commitment, we must make sure that those who become others' shepherds are personally ready for the task.

Many people grow up unprepared to enter into mutual, caring relationships with anyone. They have few if any experiences of what life can be like in a safe and loving environment. Their needs and wants were not attended to in a timely fashion. They were not a source of delight to those caring for them. They were taught neither to care about others nor to take pleasure in doing so. Their families were and perhaps are held captive by a host of forces that make it difficult for anyone in them to learn how to care for others effectively and to come to trust in themselves as reliable caregivers. Some families remain in thrall to fears for their members' survival, others to self-centered members unwilling to attend to anyone's needs other than their own, and still others to stifling rules unexamined for generations as to their credibility and cogency. Rampant in all such families are neglect, abuse, smoldering anger, and a profound sense of hopelessness.

Many people who grow up in such circumstances tend to repeat in their adult relationships the dysfunctional patterns that were the sources of their misery, no matter how hard they may try to make things different for themselves and those they care about. Thanks be to God, many who share this kind of history and need find solace and strength in the church. Rather than compound the difficulties they have by asking them to bear significant burdens on behalf of someone else, we in the church must make sure that they have good shepherds who will be available to them. Someday, with God's help and with the nurture of caring Christian communities, they can become able genuinely and effectively to give of themselves to others. For now, however, they need to be ministered unto, rather than to minister.

Training Manual

How shall we as a congregation fulfill our responsibility to select only the truly called and gifted for the ministry of shepherding? The most important answer to this question is that we must do it prayerfully. We must open ourselves first and finally to God's guidance as we seek to discern the will and calling of God in the lives of each person we may be considering for training as a lay shepherd. We must ask a similar kind of openness on the part of those considering becoming lay shepherds. Together, we pray that in all things, God's will be done.

The material in *A Pastor in Every Pew* is designed to provide a general introduction to caring from a Christian point of view and to invite its readers to consider becoming more intentional in their own caring by undergoing training as a lay shepherd. There are several possible ways to help those who may be interested in further training to discern their respective callings.

One way is to encourage discussion of the training program early in the general group study of the book. Another is to plan formal interviews before beginning a training class and to admit into it only those whose calling and gifts have been assessed by the person and by the leaders of the program. A third is to open the training to anyone interested and to assess each member's readiness to become a lay shepherd in the light of his or her participation in the training. Some churches may decide to combine one or more of these possibilities.

The one thing that needs to be communicated clearly, whatever procedure a particular church may choose to follow, is that participation in a study of *A Pastor in Every Pew* and in subsequent training are prerequisites for commissioning as a lay shepherd. But the church's decision to commission will depend on a process of mutual discernment toward the end of the training program. Training must be completed satisfactorily, and not just completed, for commissioning to be warranted.

Training Manual